Seven Essential Qualities for Spiritual Success
*Guidance from a Modern-day Spiritual Master*

© 2012 Center of The Golden One®
First Edition, 2012
Published by Center of The Golden One
4277 W. 43rd Avenue
Denver, CO 80212

Library of Congress Control number: 2010925451
ISBN: 978-1-935750-03-1
Printed in the United States of America.

# Seven Essential Qualities for Spiritual Success

Guidance from a
Modern-day Spiritual Master

*God's love*
*is the most powerful force there is.*
*God's power is love.*
*God's love is the source of everything that is.*

*You will find your true power, true joy,*
*and all abilities in the love of God.*
*Without finding your way into the heart of God,*
*you will not find your true power,*
*strength, endless love, and every other quality*
*that is born of God's love.*

KALINDI

# Kalindi

Kalindi, a powerful modern-day spiritual master, has brought forth
knowledge, guidance, inspiration, and encouragement
for the spiritual awakening happening now on the planet.

*I can help you with something that is very, very rare
to achieve – to learn how to get in touch with God in a very
real way so that you can understand His language.
And then to be able to tune in within – deep within yourself
to where you can hear Him.*

*I can help you so that you can learn to hear Him.
And so you can walk your life all the time with Him,
because He's leading the way.*

*I have so much to share with you from God
to help you in your life – in your material life and in
your spiritual life.*

KALINDI

## 5 Humility

## 6 Inner Strength

## 7 Ability to Be in Action

*The truth cannot be put into words; it cannot.*
*So everything that's coming out of my mouth to guide you*
*is to give you a hint at the direction that you*
*should go in, in order that you can directly come*
*to realize the truth for yourself.*

KALINDI

In the talks in this book, Kalindi specifically speaks to those searching for ultimate spiritual freedom, returning back Home to God in this lifetime – but the truth she speaks is for *all* who desire to strengthen their connection with the Divine and who are walking a path of becoming freer and closer to God each day.

Kalindi's guidance is meant for healthy people of sound mind who want to move closer to God. If you choose to follow Kalindi's spiritual guidance contained in this book, we urge you to do so responsibly and with full love, care, and respect for yourself and others – as this is one of Kalindi's main teachings.

For this book, Kalindi's spoken words have been edited for clarity and readability. Kalindi's original speaking of the talks in this book are available on CD at the Center of The Golden One online store (http://store.CenterofTheGoldenOne.com).

Refer to the Glossary at the back of the book (page xiii) for an explanation of people and terms used in the book.

# Essential Qualities

*Desire for God, as well as trust and faith in God,*
*are at the core of having a loving and personal relationship*
*with God. Out of desire, trust, and faith, the basis*
*of transformation – and the work – begins.*

*Supporting trust, faith, and desire are the God-given*
*qualities of courage, determination, inner strength, humility,*
*and action. By mindfully developing and applying these*
*qualities with a focus to know God, a real and dynamic*
*relationship with God will be experienced.*

*When difficulties arise – and they will – by resourcefully*
*immersing yourself in these essential qualities,*
*you will change, you will overcome obstacles, and you will*
*especially be able to remain true to your desire for God.*
*A life given in love and devotion to the pursuit of God*
*results in the joy, inner peace, and harmony of being with*
*God. It all begins with desire, trust, and faith.*

THE LADY
Kalindi's first disciple
Spiritual Master for the World

# Becoming Fully Aware is the Way Home

*Introduction by Jim St. James*

Home is real and God (Source) is real. Home is the realm where the Lord God resides. And to be fully Home[1] is true enlightenment, which is not the same as the false notion of trying to enlighten the ego. Kalindi, a spiritual master for the world, is bringing teachings which are not meant to help you strive for a mere idea of enlightenment, but instead are meant to help you find ultimate freedom and *true* awakening. This happens through God's grace, a spiritual master's guidance, and your effort, awareness, and letting go.

Home is what you draw nearer to as you become freer and freer from your ego illusions. Home is God's love, and nothing but God – and it's not a far off place in the cosmos. You cannot see it or touch it, but you can feel it. And the freer from your ego you become, the more you can feel Home.

A "state of full awareness" is another way to describe the state a person lives in when they are Home. And coming Home takes

---

[1] Being fully Home refers to a state you achieve while you are alive; it can *only* happen before death.

some time and a lot of letting go. Being *fully* Home means having to let go of all ego entirely and become unbound by the needless sufferings of the ego (anxiety, worry, hatred, fear, mistrust, loneliness, guilt, shame, and many others).

Home is what everyone ultimately wants, because the feeling of Home is total fulfillment of the heart. That is what God's love is. But our ideas of what we *think* we want get in our way. We try to satisfy our longing for God's love with material pleasure, be it sex, food, relationship, work, or whatever. Our sentimental and limited ideas of what we *think* love is get in our way of feeling the real love of God.

God knows what we each ultimately want, and at this time in our history He is giving the world what it needs to know about how to get it. This takes going within and getting free of our ego illusions. Kalindi is bringing this knowledge to us, and she is bringing us the faith in God that helps us trust enough to let go of those illusions.

Beware that the mind creates its own ideas about God's love and truth. So we need teachings and guidance to help us to not be satisfied with relying on concepts and ideas, but rather to find the *true* love of God. Kalindi's teachings help us walk a spiritual path of *true* self realization and awareness, and it cannot be stressed enough that walking a path of self realization is fundamentally different from having ideas or concepts. Many seekers think they already know this, because their intellect resonates with the truth of it. But it often takes a bit more work to let go of the idea that you even know or understand this. But if you do, then you can find actual self realization. (The trap of the material mind is so tricky; that is why a master who has navigated this territory is necessary to guide the way.)

Kalindi is bringing you teachings about how to steadily and incrementally find greater levels of self awareness, until you are all the way Home – if that is what you want – or until you achieve whatever level of self awareness that satisfies you.

Becoming fully self aware *is* becoming entirely free from the illusion – all ego. The more of your ego you let go of, the more of your truer self is realized. The more you let go, the more you become self aware. You let go, become more aware, let go, become more self aware – over and over again – according to how far your desire takes you. That is essentially the path of becoming self aware.

You achieve a state of full awareness over time by using your inherent God-given qualities to help you let go of parts of your false ego, and thus come into more of your true nature with God. In this book, Kalindi teaches you ways to use and develop your innate qualities from God. By following her guidance and direction, you can become more and more self aware and come to tangibly know and feel that you are coming closer to God. If you can sincerely immerse yourself in developing each quality, while letting go of your ego along the way, then you can come ever closer and closer to God, and you can walk as far as you like – all the way Home if you desire.

In the next chapter, in her talk "Achieving a State of Full Awareness," Kalindi introduces five innate qualities given to us by God: courage, determination, humility, inner strength, and the ability to be in action. These qualities, along with the core spiritual elements of desire, and trust and faith, are the topics for the major sections of this book. In each section, there are talks spoken by Kalindi directly guiding her disciples on a path to full awareness and ultimate freedom, Home. These talks will give you insight for utilizing your innate qualities from God on your own path of spiritual transformation.

# Achieving a State of Full Awareness

*spoken on December 16, 1995*

I've been talking to you for so long now about freedom, about God, that "everything is waiting," ultimate freedom, self-realization, enlightenment, on and on. You all have such sincere desire in your hearts. My job is to help you to break free from the illusion. One way that help comes is through my speaking to you and educating you about the illusion and how the illusion has you bound.

You see, I'm trying to pull you within so deep to come through the illusion. Come Home! Come on! Let go! Give up! Surrender! So I pull on you and you're all moving, moving, moving. And it is everything that's waiting for you.

But you need to grasp some very basic understandings in order to go forward. So I am going to go into very basic areas, subject by subject, topic by topic, for as long as it takes, to try to help you understand so that you can get free in this lifetime, so that you can succeed. My request to you is that you train yourself to listen very carefully when I speak, because everything that I say is very important for you to hear.

One of the points I want to talk to you about is that you have a concept of what self-realization, enlightenment, union with God will be like. You do not understand. You have only a dream going on. You have to let go of your idea or concept about how it's going to look or be.

I want to talk to you very, very practically now and help you gain a very, very practical understanding as you are going through transformation with the goal of union with God in this lifetime. The state that you achieve, in the end, is a state of full awareness. I want to use that term, "full awareness," because there is a very practical understanding that you can start to grasp about the daily path and about what, in the end, you're going to have in the palm of your hand.

Yes, what you will have is everything. It is God. It is the Kingdom of God within. It is enlightenment. It is self-realization. But those words aren't helping you. Even striving for that isn't helping on a day-to-day basis. Your underlying goal needs to be for ultimate freedom and truth. But I want you to wake up to very practical understandings now about your day-to-day life on your path to God, in your path with God, and in a state of full union with God. *It's all about awareness.*

You will never find a fully realized being who can't think and who doesn't see what's going on in their life, in their surroundings, in their environment, in all ways. A fully realized being has eyes and brains all around, not only fully aware in the spiritual realm, but aware in this physical reality as well – a very keen vision and ability to function, to solve problems, to see what the problem is, to come up with solutions. There is such a high level of thinking and control of the mind that goes on in a realized being – control of the mind, control of the emotions, control of the senses. As you come closer to God, your ability to think and solve problems materially and spiritually becomes sharper and sharper. You ultimately tap into such a high level of intelligence.

On a very practical level now you're coming to meditations, you're sincere, you're praying, "God, take me, take me, take me. I give You my life." And you're crying and you're praying and you're meditating and you're doing everything. I want to tell you now – listen to this: *Do not waste any time while you're using precious hours to meditate!* Don't pray to God to save you, to help you, to come to you, to release you from this illusion – don't pray to God for all that if you're not willing to take your position and role as a human being that's striving for God consciousness. As a human being, God has given you so many tools to use in order that the functioning of your life can go smoothly, in order that your spiritual quest and search for God can go smoothly. You have to use the tools that are within you. And as you awaken more and more, you will be using those tools more and more.

If you're praying for God to save you and take you, and you are praying, "I give You my life," but then you're sitting there and you can't figure out how to get any money, or your job's not working; or your life isn't working and you're just boo hoo hoo crying for God – what are you doing? You should be taking care of your life on every level as you're moving closer to God. And you'll be able to take care of your life on every level materially and spiritually if you will *think*, if you will calm down your emotions, and if you will actually think about specific areas of your life that need attention, materially or spiritually.

You're going to have the same obstacle in your material life as you have in your quest for God. It's the same game, the same illusion that's stopping you from having a job and creating income so that you are okay in life. The illusion that is stopping you from functioning and pulling it together in your life as a human being is the same illusion that you are going to run up against in your quest for God.

You have to use the tools that are within you that are your inherent qualities. As you evolve more and more toward a state of full awareness, your inherent qualities will become greater and greater and greater and greater. As you connect more and more to the divine Source, from where all qualities come, your qualities become just greater and greater. You have those qualities inside of you. So don't try to go to God to get something from Him if you're not willing to do your part and use all of your tools, all of your qualities.

For you to begin to access all of your qualities, and to start to have everything function accurately for you so that you can succeed spiritually, and so that your material life is in service to your spiritual quest, you are going to have to *think*. For you to access these qualities (which are inside of you, they're just covered by illusion) and start to get them functioning for your well-being and success, you are going to have to think. You're going to have to come up with many, many solutions in your life, forever, while you're in this human form.

Even when you're fully with God, you have to become even sharper. Your mind becomes as a yogi: very focused, very sharp. You're not in some dream bliss-land. You *are* in the divine bliss and ecstasy, but believe me, it's not like what you think. You are *so* real and you are *so* focused. You can focus on whatever your mind sets out to focus on, whether it is a material area or spiritual area. You are fully aware.

Right now you have to wake up your awareness at whatever level it's at, and it's got to start to come forth. You have to access your thinking in order to access your qualities. And you have to calm down your emotions and your senses and your mind so that you can think and have things work for you.

God will help you to access information in your meditations. But you have to ask, you have to think, you have to be focused, and you have to be a very sincere "yes." "Yes" in your conscious mind, "yes" in your subconscious mind, "yes" on all levels. The decision has to be made in you: "I am going to succeed and I am going to do whatever it takes in order to break free." You have to become a total "yes." And from that total "yes," when you hear guidance and direction, you'll start to take it. And I'm telling you, you need to *think*.

Now, do you know why you don't want to think? It's because you're too lazy. That's how the illusion has you. The illusion doesn't want you to think, because if you think, and you think everything through thoroughly, you are going to be able to break free, because you will take all of the proper steps necessary materially and spiritually to succeed. If you think, if you meditate deeply, and if you pray, the answers will come. And then you have to listen, say yes, and act. That's called "true hearing." You have to listen, say yes, and act.

You have to be willing to be in action constantly. There's no time to waste in a day. You have so much to do. There are so many things to do in your material life, and there are so many things to do on your spiritual quest. They both cross over; it's the same illusion in both areas that has you stuck. It's because of your laziness and that you haven't made the decision totally, "I'm going to do whatever it takes."

You make that decision, "I'm going to do whatever it takes," and then set yourself straight walking forward and you meditate. And you meditate with deep focus. No matter what area you're meditating on, you're very focused. And when it comes time to think, it's not like you have to figure out what you need to think about. You should be so focused every day that when it comes time to meditate, while you're driving to the meditation, you should know what you have to find a solution to. You should know what the one thing is that you need to focus on.

You have to think. It's very simple: you have to think, you have to meditate deeply, you have to be in prayer so that you can find the answers that will have you succeed both materially and spiritually. You want to succeed materially for the purpose of God, not for the purpose of becoming some great being in the illusion, but so that you can handle things in life, that you have a grip on everything, that you have sufficient funds, that you have sufficient health care, that you're taking care of your body. You should be able to think and access information about all these basic things that go on in life and then go into action. You find a solution and then simply do it.

But the illusion doesn't want you to think. The illusion would love to have you lying on the floor, meditating for years, crying, "God, God, God, I'm surrendered. Take me, take me, take me," but on your part you're never willing to go into action. Some of you use meditation and spiritual life as an escape from the reality of the human existence that you're walking in.

I'm telling you, you're going to find your way to God in this human form while you're walking here on earth. You are going to be very sharp. You are going to come to the highest human capability, highest human achievement possible, which means your mind is going to be sharp. At what point are you going to start to use your mind, your brains, your thinking, and your tools that

God has given you? At what point are you going to get every-thing to click?

There should be no excuses in your life, because if you are properly focused every day of your life and meditating proper-ly, you will be opening up, releasing, breaking illusions, and letting walls down so your heart is more open to receive God's love and truth. You'll be thinking about what you need to do. You'll be thinking about your ego and parts of your ego that need to go. You'll be thinking about your material life and what you need to do in your material life. You'll be thinking about what you need to let go of in life. You will be thinking about everything. You are going to be thinking about everything for the rest of your life even when you are one with God, fully in His Kingdom.

*While you're in this body, you are going to be thinking.* And you are just going to eventually come to a place of a full state of awareness where you are aware of the material and spiritual, where you see the distinction, where you see the crossing of the two, where you see the duality of material existence. With your intelligence, with your mind, with your prayer, and with your willingness to be in action, you're actually going to *break* the illusion – and you do this with God's help and with the guidance that comes and with your *action*.

The illusion would love you to say, "Well, I have to focus on material life, so I can't meditate or focus on spiritual life." That's the illusion too. You have to do *everything*. You have to meditate. You have to serve God. Your whole life needs to revolve around that. And you live your life as a human being in this world, taking care of all of your material affairs. You need to learn to listen and not be stopped by fear. You need to do what you need to do. And you need to have courage to take the action that you need to take in order to have things work for your success in your transformation back into God, living a life in full God consciousness.

There are many things that are going to go on in meditation. There are many levels of work going on simultaneously in your transformation. And you are going to have to think about everything so that you can solve every different problem that's going on. God will help you to access answers, *but He won't do it for you.* You have got to be in *action*, taking the right steps in order to succeed. If you don't use your tools and your qualities that are inherent in you, you won't come to a state of full awareness. It's by accessing the qualities that are within you that you will come to a state of full awareness and union with God.

I want to discuss just briefly a few qualities that you all have. Some of you think you don't have them, and that's because they are covered by illusion. So you need to pray, and you need to work hard on yourself, and you need to ask, "What can I do to uncover this quality more? Because I need this quality."

I'm going to give you five qualities now. There are *many* qualities that are within you that you are going to access as you truly say yes and take responsibility for your spiritual transformation and your material existence as a human being walking in God. As you take responsibility, you'll see. You *have to* access these qualities. You won't make it without your qualities. So you need to uncover the illusion off them, and you need to use your thinking in order to get these qualities to come into proper functioning. Then these qualities are going to develop and develop and develop and develop, and you are just going to come into more and more and more of who you are.

Of course, all the while you need to be watching because of the ego. You have so much work to do. Your mind has to be helping you. Your mind and your thinking have to start to become your best friend.

What I want to do with you now is just keep it very simple. A simple path. Step by step is how we're going to go. This is what I want you to now know from this one talk: you have to take responsibility. You have to think. God is not going to do it for you. He is going to help you and give you everything that you need, but you have to do your part. You have to use the tools He's given you. And you have to start to think.

Now here are the five qualities:

**Inner strength.** This must be found in order to travel the path Home to God and in order to travel through the rest of your human existence. You have to start to tap into your inner strength. Then you pray to God to bring you more inner strength. You look at what illusion is covering that inner strength, and you start to move the illusion. You find out what that illusion is and you pray, "What can I do to find more inner strength?" And you find it within yourself. Inner strength is a must and it lies within you.

As you uncover your inner strength and you pray for purity and no ego, God will bring you more strength. Inner strength is not power derived from the ego. It's something else.

You will start to derive very great inner strength from God, but you've got to access it first within yourself. Even if it's just a spark, you've got to access the quality within you that is true – your inner strength that is connected with God. And you have to start to walk through life with that inner strength constantly holding you.

The next quality is **determination**. Unwavering determination.

The next quality is **courage**. Courage means that you will act and do what you need to do despite the fear. Courage means you will do it anyway, even if you are afraid. You will do what you need to do. If you don't have courage, it will be very hard for you to hear information from within when you're thinking. You must find courage.

The next quality is **humility**. Without humility, the ego will survive and you will not be receptive to God's truth. Humility is *not* unworthiness. Humility comes from great inner strength, great courage, great determination. You must have a state of humility with God and when you're trying to hear truth, or you won't be able to hear. The ego will be doing the listening. You must have humility. It is within each of you, and it does not have a feeling to it of unworthiness. When you think you are in a state of humility, if you are feeling a feeling of unworthiness, then you are *not* in a state of humility. So don't confuse those two. Humility is very great truth and love within you. With humility, the death of the false self can happen.

The last quality that you must tap into is your **ability to be in action**. You need to access your inner strength, you need to access your determination, you need to access your courage, you need to access your humility, and with all of that you need to access your ability to be in action – to do what you need to do in all areas of your life, spiritually and materially, every day. *You have to be in action.*

These qualities are within you, along with many others that I'll talk about in the future.

They are going to become stronger and stronger and stronger in you as you awaken – all of them. They are all very key to your spiritual transformation.

You have to do the work. God can only help someone who will help himself. God has given you the tools. You just happen to be trapped by the illusion and are too lazy to use the tools, so you don't succeed in your endeavors, materially or spiritually. And you don't *think* in order to find *proper* solutions – proper, accurate solutions that take you closer to God and that have your life working for you for God.

So these are the qualities: inner strength, determination, courage, humility, and the ability to be in action. You should now find out which of these qualities is your weakest and start to think in your meditation how you can strengthen and bring forth that quality in yourself more. Maybe it's every area that needs strengthening. And I'm telling you: don't waste time in meditation!

In your daily life you're giving so much to God. Now give God – and give yourself – the gift of your inherent qualities so that you can become a being of God's love in this world. Find your qualities! Use the tools! Uncover the illusion! Think! Wake up!

I hope that this is clear. Listen to this talk many times. There is no excuse other than your laziness. It's your fault if something is not working. If you're not coming closer to God, it's your fault. If your life isn't working materially, it's your fault. All help and all ability are there for you if you will just have the total "Yes, I will do whatever it takes to break free of the illusion." Then you walk the straight path toward truth, toward love, toward God, toward honesty – every day freer and freer, every day doing what you need to do in all areas of your life.

*Everything* needs to be paid attention to. Everything. And you don't do one without the other; you don't do the material without the spiritual, or vice versa. You do everything *simultaneously.*

Now you can meditate about how much thinking you are going to have to do. How wonderful that you actually have the gift of the ability to think and access intelligence. With that, you can access the *source* of your intelligence – which is more intelligence, which will bring you more awareness, which will ultimately bring you to a full state of awareness. But you will not achieve a full state of awareness, which is enlightenment, without accessing these qualities that are within you.

There is no escaping reality in order to find reality. In other words, you cannot escape from your material human condition and try to run into God and be irresponsible and not pay attention. You're going to be paying attention to your material existence the whole time you are in this body. When you are fully in a state of total bliss and ecstasy, you are paying attention to everything, both spiritually and materially. You become like a yogi. Your mind is so sharp, so clear. Your senses are so controlled. Your emotions are so calm through the emotional release that you are learning in the meditation. You learn how to release so that you can calm and so that you can open up.

I want to stop now. I think I've given you enough. Who of you listened while I spoke? And who of you will now get this talk and listen to it many times and actually go into proper action so that you can succeed in achieving a state of full awareness in this lifetime?

Thank you for listening. I pray for you that you will hear.

# Desire

*Desire is everything.*

GOURASANA

*Knock, and the door will be opened.*
*Knock from your soul. Knock from your desire.*
*God answers desire.*
*If you want to be with Him,*
*to whatever degree you want that,*
*to that degree it will happen.*
*And if you want it purely, with just 100% truth,*
*and that is your prayer, and you are willing,*
*then guess what?*
*You are going to be helped to find that result.*
*However much you want God,*
*however much you want to let go,*
*that is how much you are going to find.*

KALINDI

# Desire Is Everything

*spoken on February 4, 1996*

I would like this to be a talk with which you can find encouragement and inspiration in times that you are doing well, and in times that you are having difficulties.

You have heard me say that desire is everything. I have put so much emphasis on building your desire into intense desire, because it is by intense desire that you will be able to break free.

So many of you have burning, intense desire. Not just the people on this path, but all seekers. All people in the world who are seeking God have intense desire. There is great desire for God going on at this time in this world. That desire itself, that intense desire, that burning desire, is your prayer. Whether you speak a prayer in words or not, desire itself – as you feel it inside of you – is prayer. God doesn't necessarily hear words, although the words can help you access the feeling inside of you. It is the heartfelt, soulfelt feeling inside of you that actually communicates with God.

As you are consumed more and more by desire for love, for light, for truth, and for consciousness, God hears that desire and assists you according to your desire. This is one thing to really understand: God is assisting everyone according to what their desire is – not according to what your mind wants, or what you think you want, but what the heart of your desire is, on a soul-felt level.

Your level of desire depends on what consciousness you are in, what state of evolution you are in within the material world. God is responding to the deepest desire in your heart that is driving you. So if your desire is for love, for truth, for light, for freedom from the illusion, for love of God, then the assistance that is coming in right now – a very special, very powerful assistance – will help you more and more as it becomes your desire to be free, to be with God, to be in His light and love. God wants to help you to move as rapidly as you can, but He can only help you according to your desire.

For those of you who wonder if you are praying, or wonder how to pray, you can know that your intense desire, your desire itself, is prayer. The feeling, the longing in your heart, that nagging feeling, the frustration that you are not going fast enough, that you want more, that you want to break through, the desire that you feel for completion – that driving, underlying feeling you feel – that is prayer.

Just take a moment and feel in yourself how much of the day you are actually in prayer. Most of the people listening to this talk can feel the degree of desire that is within their being.

You want to get to the point where you desire God, truth, and love more than you desire anything else. You want to get to the point where you desire God's love, true love, real love, unending love, full light, consciousness, knowledge, awareness, a full state of awareness free from the illusion, more than you desire anything else. This doesn't mean you can't engage in activities of this world. You will be engaging in activities of this world while you are in this world, but you can be engaging in all the various activities while still having desire to be living in light, in truth, and in God's love. That desire, that constant prayer, never has to go away.

For many of you, if you just focus within for a minute, you will see, "I do have that desire all the time, and it's becoming greater each day. As I desire it more, I am moving faster. More consciousness is coming to me. More awareness is coming to me. More openness is happening for me. More connection is happening with me because of my desire and my willingness to move forward as God is helping me."

Your desire is your prayer. That is a barometer you can use inside of yourself: What is your desire? Are you going sometimes for a week without any desire for consciousness, or love, or light, or God? Or are you focused on God, truth, love, light, freedom every day? And if it is every day, what portion of the day?

Desire doesn't mean that in your conscious mind you are constantly thinking about desire. Desire comes from a deeper, more feeling place inside of you. You can be engaged in work and other activities in your daily life, but you can feel a part of you that is dissatisfied. You can feel a part of you that longs for something more. That feeling of dissatisfaction is a type of desire. It is a type of prayer that is going on constantly. To be in a constant state of prayer and desire doesn't mean that in your conscious mind you are always thinking of desire. Desire doesn't mean that your consciousness is always going to be thinking of desire. It means, rather, that you have a feeling inside of desire for freedom all of the time. Then slowly, slowly, slowly, as you are willing, God can pull you through different parts of the illusion, because it is your desire.

God can only answer your desire. It is your desire that is creating separation and that had you come to experience the material world of illusion in the first place. God assisted that desire. It is because of your desire that you are going to get out of the material illusion with His assistance. The assistance from God to help you break free is very great and it is available at this time on the planet.

You can allow your desire to build and grow, until every single day, twenty-four hours a day, you are consumed by desire for truth and for God consciousness. Again, it doesn't mean that your desire is in your mind. It is more of a feeling that you walk in. It is more of an awareness that you walk in.

You come to a point where you understand that you cannot be complacent. Until you are carried away by the presence of the Lord, do not rest. You will come to a point where you feel that in yourself. Do not be satisfied to stay in the illusion any longer. Do not be complacent. And do not rest your endeavor until you find yourself immersed in the love of God. Through your choice, through your desire, through your conscious awareness, you will come to the point when you live your life in such a way that you are constantly moving forward every day as much as you can, moving through illusions, letting go of illusions.

The illusion doesn't all go in one day. You move through as much as you can every day, so that at the end of every day you can feel, "So much happened today. So much happened in my consciousness. I've changed so much in one day." Some of you may recognize the change and some of you may not. Some of you may be in the midst of movement, and when you are in the midst of movement, you are thinking most of the time that something is wrong. You are thinking that you are not making progress. You have to change that consciousness a little bit, because when you are in the midst of movement and a change in consciousness, and you are letting go of illusions, often you feel like you are getting nowhere and you are going backwards, when in fact it is just a matter of time before you break through into more light.

Desire is everything. You want to get to the point where the desire is with you, and you feel that current of desire running through your system all of the time. If you desire to totally be free of the illusion and enter into a state of full awareness, total awareness, then your desire is a prayer. And that prayer is immediately answered. God is doing everything that He can do to help guide your every step, so that you can find your way through the illusion. Your prayer is answered.

Some of you have already reached this point of wanting God and nothing else. Some of you are well on your way. Want God and nothing else, and then you will come face-to-face with the Lord. You will. And He is just waiting for you to want Him. He is waiting for you to want truth and love so badly that you want it above and beyond anything else.

No matter how many realizations you have, no matter how many experiences you have, no matter how far you have come on the path, and no matter how free you are of the illusion, you need to be situated in a consciousness of constant movement forward. God, by nature, is an ever-increasing force, and you want to be moving, in God, always ready for more of God.

So, do not be satisfied or complacent, or be hooked into individual spiritual experiences. Although you want to receive experiences as they come, you also want to have deep desire going on within that experience, "Yes, it's wonderful that there is a realization that this connection is happening with the light and love, but I want it all, so let me have this and then let me let it go." Let the experiences go. Have the realizations and change because of the realizations. Then let your desire call more of God to you, until you truly are carried away by the presence of the Lord, by the feeling of God constantly taking you ever closer, ever closer, into His nature.

Desire to be free from the illusion. And you know what? Then desire it more, until you are consumed by desire. I am speaking this to you, and I hope that this talk will bring encouragement to you, because so many of you are already consumed by desire. If you come to that point where you have no other desire but to find the love, the light, the truth (which is all waiting for you right now), then recognize what a great blessing it is that you have this consciousness going on. Because this consciousness, this desire, will guarantee that you take the necessary steps. It will guarantee your success. God will answer you because of that desire. You will pray. You will search for truth. And then you will act upon what you need to do to break free. The desire is everything, and the desire guarantees your success.

Now you also have to go into action and let go. You cannot hang on to the illusion. You have to let go. And you need to come to a point in your spiritual endeavor that you don't become discouraged, and that you never give up. The main thing is that you never give up. As long as you continue moving forward and continue trying, whether your conscious mind can understand or not, you are growing at a very rapid rate within that intense desire. This is true whether you consciously know it or not. It may take five years for you to awaken to what has happened to you, to understand the degree of growth you have had, but at some point it will all blossom for you, and your mind will be aware of it.

For some of you there might be hard times during transformation. Do not look upon that as something bad. If you look at the hard time that is going on and you drop into your feeling, you will see that you have nothing but desire going on. So, maybe then you can interpret this hard time as something good: "There is movement going on. I am moving forward. There is nothing wrong, and at some point this will open up and blossom into more love and more light." So, don't be discouraged on your path.

One of the secrets to spiritual movement is constant change. You are going to be doing either one of two things: you are going to be in service to the illusion or in service to God. So, you can be changing – and your consciousness can be changing to bring you into more and more illusion, or your consciousness can be changing to bring you into more and more light. You want to change, and you want to change into truth, into consciousness, into light. You do not want to step into more illusion, or another role of illusion, or another type of illusion with your consciousness. Step into more light.

It takes time to become free of interacting in the illusion. It takes a little time to let illusions fall away and to become truly situated in light in this world. It is something that happens step by step by step. The illusion starts to fall away; you start to not want to participate as much in illusory activities, because you find a greater type of pleasure from living in consciousness in this world.

This doesn't mean you can't have fun and you can't have pleasure. When I talk about living in the light and in truth rather than in the illusion, you will tend to think that I mean that you will no longer do anything in this world because it is all illusion. That is not what I mean, and I can't really explain what I mean; it is something that you just need to experience. There are so many things now that you just no longer have the desire for. For example, some of you no longer have the desire to party in the way that you used to party. Perhaps you used to drink alcohol and have fun, like in college. It is something that you just don't want to do anymore. You have grown out of it. You are also going to grow out of the illusion, but you will still be able to have different pleasures. You will choose to do things for pleasure that don't disturb your consciousness. You will choose to do things that actually are running alongside with where you are in your consciousness.

I just wanted to encourage you a little bit by talking about desire. I will share with you personally about the beginning of my own transformation. My transformation began when I was eighteen years old. At a certain point in 1987, Gourasana said to The Lady and me that we had to get to the point where we had desire and prayer twenty-four hours a day. We looked at each other and we thought, "What does that mean? How is that possible?" We would pray when we meditated, but we didn't know what it meant to live consciously, in prayer and desire. But Gourasana told us, "You will see. You will come to that point."

Then he told The Lady to get one of these egg timers that have sand in them, that you can turn upside down, and wear it around her neck and turn it over when it ran out. He said that would be a way that she could be constantly returning to her desire. Every time she turned it over, she could pray and return herself to her desire for God. That is where we came up with the idea of having people wear watches that beep every hour, so that at least for one minute every hour, you can return yourself to a conscious prayer. That is where that started. Very quickly our desire became so intense that we started to understand what He meant. It didn't take too long until we were just consumed, daily, with desire and prayer.

It is really true that your desire is what will set you free. God answers your desire. It's really true. There is so much power coming in from God right now, a very special assistance to help you break free. You can call upon that assistance from God, the very powerful energy that is coming in right now, to help you.

So, the main thing to remember is that you will succeed by your desire. If you want the love and the light of God, if you want to live in truth, then no matter how great the obstacle, no matter what it is that you have to confront and push through, you will succeed. It can be done. It can be done, and it is based upon your desire. And so many of you are well on your way. There is a way for everyone to be free of this illusion, and it begins with your desire. And your desire is answered by God's special assistance and your willingness to let go.

So, don't be complacent. Don't be complacent at any point of your path. Also, don't beat yourself up that you are not doing enough and you are not doing it fast enough. You need to be recognizing the desire that you do have while you are pushing forward. Until you are carried away by the presence of the Lord, don't rest. Don't stop your endeavor. Don't be satisfied to stay in the illusion any longer. If you want to break free, you can break free. Help is here. Assistance is here. And you are to a point in your evolutionary process where you are actually ready for that leap in consciousness to break free from the material world, to finally break free from the illusion. Desire is everything. And God is on the move to respond to your desire.

# The Longing Is the Love

*spoken on March 11, 1996*

In entering into the illusion and separating from God – going through that original separation from God, from truth, from that full connection, from your Home – in separating from that full connection, there has come along with that separation the very tool that you need in order to return to your full self in God once again.

This material creation, this illusion, this place of separation, is only meant to be temporary. Human existence itself means separation. There is no getting around it. There is separation in the material world. It is a place of separation. Though you can't remember, from the beginning as you separated from God, you knew at some point you would awaken and return to your true self in God, Home, the true realm of existence, Spirit, and no longer be entangled in separation in any way.

By entering into the illusion, you have gone through that original separation from God, from truth, from that full connection, from your Home. In separating from that full connection, you also have the very tool that you will need in order to return to your full self in God once again.

The built-in tool that you brought with you when you entered into the illusion is something called "longing." That longing is the driving force that is inside of everyone. No matter what level of evolution you are on, there is a longing in the heart of everyone that goes unfulfilled despite efforts to create happiness or pleasure or comforts or love in the material world. Despite what you have and what you have achieved in this material world, deep in your heart there is a longing that cannot be satisfied with anything less than your true self in God once again; you returning back to God.

This longing carries you through your entire journey in the material existence. Your longing is what propels you from one lifetime to the next, to the next, to the next. It is your constant search for that one thing that you can't remember because, in your state of separation, you have forgotten. Your longing keeps pushing you forward in search of something until you finally have enough consciousness to understand that no matter how good everything is that you experience of this material world, there is still a nagging longing in your heart, in your soul, that goes unfulfilled.

It is that very longing that is the tool that eventually will pull you all the way out of material existence, back Home, back to your origin. In order to return Home, you will cross through the pain of separation. With that longing, you will cross back through the pain that you felt when you separated from God. The longing is what takes you there, that longing inside of you that is never fulfilled. Eventually that longing becomes strong enough that nothing but full awareness and full connection to God will satisfy it. Only full and complete endless love of God and your eternal relationship again with God will satisfy that longing – no more illusion. The longing is your tool.

In the beginning of your spiritual transformation, you are going through so many surface issues that cause you pain as you are letting go and as you are transforming. But as you understand the longing more and more, as you trust and go deeper and deeper within, you will hit upon the longing in its depth. The longing at its core, the longing in its depth, is your love for God and God's love for you. It is the thread between you and God that pulls you Home.

Everyone is very afraid to feel the longing in its depth, because it is so painful to feel the depth of that longing. But it is inside the very depth of that longing that you feel your incredible desire and love for God and want to return to God. You start to feel God pulling on you to come, come Home, come back. It is difficult to enter into the core of the longing. And along the way, as you're searching for that core longing, you will tap into more surface issues that may cause you to be sidetracked. You may get sidetracked into wallowing, self-pity, unworthiness, blame, and shame – just some of the issues of the illusion that you are working through.

You want to be careful, as you are going within in search of your deeper longing, that you are not getting trapped in deep emotions and deep pain of these surface issues without tapping into the deeper longing. You want to eventually go beyond and beneath all of the surface issues into the core longing, where you know that nothing but God will satisfy you. God starts to hear you when you're in the depth of that longing, and He starts to answer you, and He starts to pull you out of the material illusion back into the light and love.

The longing is the love; it's your love for God and it's God's love for you. It's the thread that will pull you out of material existence back to Him fully.

The separation from God is the most painful thing to feel, worse than any other physical or mental pain possible in the material world. Worse than anything is to feel the pain of the separation. And in order to get to the core of your longing, in order to connect again to that thread that will take you Home, you will have to cross through that separation.

The longing is the love. The longing will pull you back to God. But you need to surrender to the longing. You need to understand from a very positive place that the longing, in its depth – as painful as it may feel because of the separation – is the very tool that will help you to get out of the illusion and return to God. In the beginning of your transformation, the loneliness that you feel is the beginning of that feeling of longing, but it is still on a surface layer. That is why you need to travel always deeper and deeper within to get to the core longing. When you get to that core longing, your prayer through and through will be to God, "Please help me. I want to be with You again."

You will learn prayer when you find your longing. You will learn how to pray from such a depth that God does hear your prayer. And He answers you. Within your loneliness, even in the surface state of the beginnings of your feeling of loneliness, there is a longing to return to the eternal, unending relationship of love with the Lord.

At times you have to go through much despair to find the depth of your longing. As you go deeper and deeper, you will come to realize that nothing of the sense pleasures of this world – no matter how good they get – will satisfy that longing. There is nothing wrong with participating in sense pleasures; you just need to do it with awareness. You need to understand, if you are searching for freedom and for God, these sense pleasures are not bringing you the satisfaction that your soul is searching for. They are not bringing you the fulfillment of your longing that is crying out. They never will. At most they are just a band-aid to cover up the "ouch" of the loneliness and the despair that you are feeling in the moment. Those of you that have the courage will go to the depth of your longing, and you won't leave that depth until God answers your longing, until God Himself picks you up.

Of course, there are many things you need to do on your path, not just feel your longing. Giving, of course, is going to be your saving grace. To give God's light and love as you are transforming is essential. Giving must be there. You won't be able to tolerate the feeling of your longing if you are not becoming a vessel of giving; the illusion will capture you in your longing – just turn into hopeless despair with no way out. Your giving, your living to give and serve, is what will help you to get through the longing. It is what will pull God's light to you and bring you back into your connection with God.

Eventually you will come to understand that the longing is the love of God. It is a very deep realization to really, truly understand that. It is difficult for people to surrender to that depth of longing without trying to have a band-aid to fix it, to have something of the senses to cover over that horrible feeling of loneliness and despair. But it is inside of that where you will find your true prayer.

I want to say a few things to you that Gourasana spoke about prayer:

> Along the path, you need to know that prayer is the most powerful tool. You can always pray. When you're lost, when you are confused, and when you

don't understand what is happening to you at all, you can always remember that prayer is a most powerful tool. No matter what your state, no matter what your situation, you can pray[1].

As you pray, God is hearing you – even though you may not know that He's on His way to answering you, and you don't know how it is that He will answer you. You can always pray. You get to the point where you pray so deeply that your life becomes a prayer. Not necessarily words formed in your conscious mind, but deep in your heart. It's like a constant seeking, a constant asking, a constant desire to know the truth, and it's a constant prayer to be free from the illusion that binds you.

Pray for the experience that you need – to bring you closer to God – to come to you, whatever that may be. And pray that you will know the truth directly. Pray to God. You can always pray. You can pray constantly to know the truth and to find the truth. How many will pray to God, will pray to the Lord? And to pray to the Lord becomes even more personal. But how many will ask Him for His help, really ask Him for His help? You'll find your true power when you find the Lord. And you will never know your true power unless you find the Lord.

How many people will go deep into the longing and into deep prayer, and from the depth of your soul cry out and beg God for mercy to hear you? He is just waiting to hear that from you; He will answer you if you want Him. But you have got to find your depth and your true desire to want God purely. And you have got to cry out for God, whether it's with silent tears of deep prayer, or whether you are actually deeply crying. You can beg God and

---

[1] See Gourasana, *Breaking the Cycle of Birth and Death*, Miracle of Love, 4th Edition, 2007, Quote #12.

DESIRE

cry to God without a tear, just in a very deep sober state, and you can cry and really release into deep crying for God.

This type of deep crying for God is not wallowing; wallowing is a trap of the illusion. (Sometimes, though, you just need to cry to release, and that is okay.) Prayerful longing is a type of crying that brings you closer to God. When you hit that depth of prayer and crying, there is a part of you that knows that God has heard your prayer and that He will start to work with you. There is a part of your soul that knows that God has heard you, and then your transformation starts to speed up, and He starts to answer your prayer. And then your longing increases, and your prayer goes deeper. Don't fear the longing. Don't be afraid to pray from your depth, because He will answer you. And don't fear your cry, the cry of your soul for union.

You see, so long ago everyone was Home. This is a little story Gourasana told me once: So long ago, you all went out to play, and your parents said "Go play, and play as long as you like. And when you're ready, come home and be comforted; come back in, because it will get wet, it will get cold. You will get sick while you're playing; you will get hurt out there all alone without your parents. So try not to forget." But what has happened in the separation is that everyone forgot that they just went out to play in a world that is a playground, where there is so much suffering. Even the happiness is mixed with suffering. It is a playground where the parents allow all of the children to go out and play for as long as they want. The parents are sitting there constantly beckoning, never for a moment forgetting the children, and feeling all of the pain and suffering that the children are going through while they are playing in the playground, then watching and seeing how the illusion has covered over all the children. And the only way that the children can find their way back home is to get to the point where the

36

playground no longer interests them, where they've outgrown the playground and the temporary happiness followed by the distress. When they've outgrown it, they start to search and long for home again. It starts to happen.

And then you start to remember your Father, your eternal Father, the Mother, the Great Mother. You start to feel that there is a place called Home, and then you start to long for that, even though you don't know it is what you are longing for, because you still don't remember that there is such a place as Home. But ever since the children went out to play, God is beckoning constantly. The parents have been sitting home saying "Come home; it's too cold out there now. You're getting hurt too many times. Come home, come home."

God's pull is constant, but He has given free will; He has answered your desire to go out and play for as long as you want. But the pull from the parents and the love from the parents is unconditional, and they sit patiently waiting for when each child is ready to come Home – to be embraced in the love and comfort of the eternal love of their Home, to come out of the cold, to come out of the dark, to come out of the illusory playground, to come within deep enough to find that Home again. And after finding that Home again, be released into self realization, and then still standing in this world of illusion, but no longer separate from Home or the parents, the Father, the Great Mother; they are no longer separate, completely whole again, self-realized, and standing in this playground of illusion to help others to find their way out of the cold, help others come within and find their way Home.

When you are living your last lifetime in a self-realized state walking in this world of illusion, you walk in so much love and ecstasy and completion within yourself. You can participate in whatever areas of the illusory pleasures are helpful to your existence for your continued few years here. There is nothing wrong with the pleasures of this world; there is only something wrong with the pleasures if they keep you in separation. So if you will just come in from the playground and return Home, then you will be able to stand in this world understanding the longing, understanding the material creation, understanding the illusion, understanding the perfection, and living your life to help other people find their way through the longing back to God, back Home.

Trust the longing in your heart. In the beginning, it just may feel like loneliness and despair that you are very afraid to go into. But if you will go beneath the surface of the wallowing, if you will cross through the fear and go through layer after layer of illusion, you will come to the longing and the prayer that will call God to you, and God will assist you in returning Home. He is responding to your desire. If you want to play in the illusion, He will let you do that. And if you want to come Home, He is there patiently waiting. When you are ready, He will send the proper help to you.

So follow the longing. Pray and cry for God. Everything is waiting, and it's the eternal "Everything." You will come to understand this, as you start to fully realize yourself in God. It is a process of self realization, and it is a very intense transformation. You need to embrace it as the greatest gift bestowed upon you. You are traveling a path of true spiritual transformation, a path to full spiritual awakening, all the way back to God. So embrace your transformation. The longing will pull you out of the material world back to God if you surrender to it. It is love.

# One Truth – Desire Is Everything

*spoken live at the 2008 Retreat on August 29, 2008*

I have one truth that I would like to say: "Desire is everything."

Because if you do not have intense desire, you will not do what it takes to break free of the illusion. It is the hardest thing to do. It takes focus every day. And it takes very deep prayer to God, Almighty Father.

That prayer has to get to the point that it's constant. And the depth of that prayer has to get deeper every day. And you have to be willing to do whatever it is to have that connection with God become complete.

I just want to bring in this one thing at this Retreat, because it's so important; I want you to just take this one thing home with you.

Desire. Where is your desire now? ... And now? ... And again, now? How strong is your desire?

It is a process that you have to go through your whole life. That's why desire is everything – because if you desire, you will do it, and nothing will stop you because your desire is everything. So I want you to contemplate that: Desire is everything.

If you have intense desire, then you're going to do whatever it takes to come closer and closer to God and freer and freer, every day of your life. I can't say that enough times. And so you have to keep coming to meditation.[1] You can't do it without the spiritual help of those that have gone before you and those that are going with you – you cannot. You'll stop so fast. Your intense desire will go away so fast if you are not in the proper association of others that are doing the same thing you are – coming into the light with the desire to stay in the light.

Try to hear what I've said, and listen again and again.

---

[1] Kalindi is referring to coming to group meditations, which are held weekly at the worldwide Centers and the community meditation locations.

# Trust and Faith

*No matter how advanced you get,*
*you always need trust and faith.*

*You come to trust*
*that place of knowing in you*
*that lives in trust and faith in God,*
*and as you let go, little by little,*
*you start to have more faith in your trust*
*because you see the results*
*of your forward movement*
*and the breakthroughs*
*that you make into the light*
*because you had trust and faith.*

KALINDI

# Trust and Faith

*spoken on February 15, 1996*

I want to talk to you about two of the most important elements you need to develop if you are to succeed in returning to full God consciousness, self realization, union with God, breaking free in this lifetime. Those two things are trust and faith.

You need to have trust and faith in God that God is moving you forward, that God is doing the needful and bringing to your life the necessary movement for your transformation back to Him. Trust and faith are not part of anything you could figure out with your mind; they are not part of your mind. I can't even say they are part of your consciousness. Trust and faith don't really even come from your heart. Where do trust and faith come from? Trust and faith are beyond your own understanding. That's why they are called trust and faith.

You have to have trust and faith to move forward into God. Having trust and faith to move forward into God means having rapid movement, rapid change, and letting go of everything that you hold to be real or true so that you can find truth within. You can't find the truth within by hanging on. What do you have to hang on to? Everyone wants to hang on to something. If you are going to make it Home, you are going to have to rely on your trust and faith.

Trust and faith are tools of the spiritual world. They come from God. They are not of this world. You can't touch trust and faith. They are immaterial. You can't perceive trust and faith with your five senses. They are beyond your mind. They really do come from your true self that is situated in God. I have to say that trust and faith are beyond your heart also, because your heart is so often affected by your mind, your thoughts, and your fears. Trust and faith are very intangible, and they are something that you come to trust. You come to trust that place of knowing within you that lives in trust and faith in God. And as you let go, little by little, you start to have more faith in your trust, because you see the results of your forward movement and the breakthroughs that you make into the light because you had trust and faith. These two basic elements that are beyond the material world, beyond even your heart, come from your true self in God.

You need to have trust and faith in God, and God will bring to you more trust and faith. It is your self that is with God already that has trust and faith. It is your true self that is with God that has trust and faith to trust the process of deep transformation in which you have to break all judgments, concepts, and beliefs in order to be with God. It is your true self in God that has trust and faith when there is nothing to hang on to.

So many times on the path you will have nowhere to turn, and you have to simply let go. The only way you will be able to do that is with trust and faith. Otherwise, you will get stuck in your mind trying to figure it out, and think about what is going on, and question, "Should I or shouldn't I let go?" Or, "What is this?

What is that? What is happening to me now? What kind of inner movement and change is going on now?" Either you are controlling the situation with your mind and saying "no" to God, or you are living in trust and faith knowing that God is directly working with you. You do know. You know from a place inside that knows, and you learn to live in trust and faith in God. Your true self has total trust and faith.

You need to get to understand the feeling of what your true self feels like versus your ego self. Your true self trusts beyond the mind. Your true self trusts even when you do not understand. Your true self knows God. Your true self knows, "God is doing this to me, for me." Your true self does not insist on controlling everything. Your true self lives in trust and faith and allows God's flow to move you forward.

As you have greater and greater trust and faith, you start to pray from a deeper place to God, "Take me faster." And God hears that prayer, "Take me faster." When you are saying that from a very true place, and when He comes to take you faster, you have sufficient trust and faith, and you let go, and you move faster. He comes. You say "yes." You let go. You have trust and faith in the way God is moving you forward.

True spiritual transformation back to God requires so much trust and faith. It is what will hold you through all of the pains and fears of letting go. It is your trust and faith that will always show you the way into more light, not your mind and your control. Your trust and faith in God moves you, not your mind and your control, because your trust and faith is with God.

You will develop greater and greater trust and faith as you let go and see that you trusted. You didn't understand, you broke through, and now there is more truth and more light. Every time that happens, you will start to feel the part of you that trusts God more, that has more faith, and you will start to live your life in trust and faith. You won't live in so much doubt about how God moves you, and how God works, and what God does to break illusions in your life.

You are asking for freedom. You are praying to God. That means He has to break the illusions and help you to break the bondage, and He will, but you have to have trust and faith in His mighty ways and in the mystery of the way that He moves you. Until you let go, you don't understand what the light is that is waiting for you.

A spiritual seeker who wants God has to learn to live in trust and faith. You can pray to God for trust and faith. And you can pray for more trust and faith. Pray to know when God is pulling, when God is pushing, when God is asking something of you. Pray to know when He is asking you to let go, to give up, to surrender, to perhaps do something for Him in service to Him. You can pray to God to give you more trust and faith to surrender to Him in whatever way He is working with you. Trust and faith is the only way to go.

Spiritual movement, rapid spiritual movement back to God, is faster than your mind can comprehend. You have to live in trust and faith if you are going to make it. Otherwise your fear and your mind will stop you, and your control will hold you back from the forward movement that is necessary. You won't understand from your mind what the "eternal everything" is that God is trying to give to you. When I say, "Everything is waiting. Let go, give up and surrender. Have trust and faith in God," you need to understand that you cannot comprehend at all the "everything" that I'm talking about. I can't even explain it to you, but it is everything.

When I say, "Everything is waiting," the only thing your mind can do with that is create a concept of what you think it will be like to be free, to be enlightened, to be in bliss. Maybe you have a picture of some past saint or master, or you have a feeling or an idea or a concept of how you think that that saint or master who was with God was feeling. Perhaps it is based on something that they said or the teachings they spoke. You have concepts that you have formed about what it feels like to be free, perhaps even based on an experience that you have had yourself.

You have nothing but concepts when I say, "Everything is waiting." You have a spiritual concept of what you think that "everything" is going to look like and feel like. So you either hook into thinking about what you are going to end up being like and feeling like and how it is all going to look spiritually, or when I say, "Everything is waiting," and "It's love and ecstasy beyond your comprehension," then your mind starts to think, "Well, what could be the greatest thing that could end up being there, that is everything?" You think of it from a material point of view. What is the greatest material pleasure? The perfect relationship? No more suffering, no more pain, no more loneliness? Then you have everything with that package fit perfectly, and you think perhaps that is what I mean by "Everything is waiting." You have a material concept of what you think "everything" is.

Your spiritual concept of what you think bliss or enlightenment is and your material concept of what you think the "everything" is are both wrong. The key thing for you to understand in this talk is, *it is beyond your comprehension.* You cannot understand it. You cannot figure it out. You have to let go, and you have to arrive, and you have to keep going because there is no end to God. So you end up living in a state of surrendered "let go," fully open, with no resistance, surrendered to the will of the Lord.

On your path, you live in trust and faith because you cannot comprehend what He is doing to break you free. So you have to have trust and faith. When you are with Him, you cannot comprehend Him at all and His many and mighty ways, and you live in full surrender within trust and faith. There you are in the flow of God: full trust, full faith, fully surrendered, moving in the one will of God. That is your freedom. The whole way from being a seeker to becoming an enlightened being, you live in surrender and in trust and faith.

You will come to understand trust and faith more and more as you directly experience them. You had trust and faith, you let go, and you broke through to greater truth and light and more love. So your direct experience of trust and faith will come to give you the trust and faith that you need in order to move into a constant state of trust and faith. Trust and faith come from your true self that is with God. Your true self does understand the letting-go process to return to God. The whole process is done with consciousness and great maturity. This is not a process of blind followers. It is a process, a path, that takes great trust and faith because God is directly moving you, and you come to understand the way that He works. You come to understand the illusion and how bound you are and that you need to move out of the illusion. And it takes great trust and faith to do this.

There will come a point when your trust and faith really click in, and that is a state of consciousness, a state of being, that you should pray to God to develop. Pray for the consciousness of trust and faith so that you can just move forward. As God calls you, say "yes."

It is not going to fit into your conscious understanding. It is not. The movement into Him, the movement with Him is all beyond your comprehension. It is all beyond your comprehension.

Who you truly are is living in trust and faith and is fully surrendered. So you want to find your true self. You can start to find a little part of your self by tapping into your trust and faith and your true surrender to God.

# God's Longing

*spoken on June 1, 1996*

One thing that you need to understand is that every single being in this material creation is evolving toward God, toward light, toward love. Every one is evolving: the bum, the drunk, the churchgoer, and the rapist. Every single path, every religion is helping people to grow, to evolve. It may not look like evolution when someone is in so much darkness, but everyone is moving toward the light at varying speeds. Even if people are in a belief system that is very stuck, even though their path itself is just a belief system or is no longer alive or helping much, their endeavor for God is moving them forward. Everyone is evolving, everyone. It is just a matter of when you are ready for full illumination, 100 percent truth. When you are ready for that, then the illusion has to die.

Every dream, every illusion, every thought that keeps you part of this illusory plane must dissolve. It is very rapid movement to go through the process of the disintegration of the ego, the false self. When you are ready for that leap in consciousness – the complete death of the ego, the false being – that is when you must have a spiritual master and a path specifically to guide you out of the illusion back into true existence, the true realm. The true realm is not the illusion at all, and it is not a concept that you come to know. It is full realization, the self in God.

You have to find a spiritual master and a path current to the age. There needs to be special power from God accompanying that master. Most often masters can't break people free. They don't have the necessary power. That has been the case in the past with most masters. Though they themselves have achieved freedom or states of freedom, they don't have the necessary power or understanding to actually help others to break free fully. The uniqueness of this Path is the power of the Incarnation Lord Gourasana, who has brought special energy, very special assistance to help those people who desire freedom in this lifetime. He has brought two spiritual masters to speak, to stand in His presence, to bring the necessary guidance, and to be a link to the Incarnation, to that presence of God as it has ushered into this world.

If you don't want full illumination, you do not need a spiritual master. If you will settle for 99 percent light – which is a lot of light and a lot of love and a better life while you live, and that is good enough for you – then you don't need a master. If a lot of God consciousness, a lot of truth, a lot of light, a lot of care, a lot of love, living your life as a human being in a wonderful way is enough for you, and you don't want full illumination, then you don't need a master. You can carry on in the dream of this illusion with your light and your love. But if you do want full illumination, to return Home, you must have a master who is specifically here for that purpose: to break you free of all illusion, no rebirth – it is very rare for someone to achieve this.

When you find that master and you are ready, you have to surrender to the path and the guidance that is the embodiment of that master. You have to surrender fully. So, if you find such a master – which is very rare – you have to surrender 100 percent to God or you won't break free. The illusion knows how to trap you in every way at every moment.

In the end, it is very simple for those of you who are serious. When you are done kicking and screaming and throwing a fit, this is what it boils down to: this material illusion is not your Home. It is not permanent. It was never meant to be eternal. And when you are ready to get out, help is brought.

God has brought to the world Kalindi, The Lady, and other leaders who will start to manifest – you watch – and His special assistance, all to guide you Home.

Do you want out of the prison, or are you willing to stay longer and continue in the drama and fantasy that this world can bring you any happiness at all? The happiness that you find in this world, at best, is still riddled with suffering. Try to understand that point. That is the nature of this material existence – suffering and separation until you break out of the illusion.

If you are serious, listen to my words, follow the guidance, give 100 percent surrender and effort on your part, and beg God, the Almighty, for mercy and grace. And never give up. Don't even consider giving up, even when you want to run because you are feeling the annihilation of the ego inside, and at times it is so frightful. Don't even consider giving up until you are Home free, in union with the Lord, no separate will.

You will unite with your master and all others who have found their way, all of the saints, all of the beings who are in God. You will be with them all. And eventually everyone will come, united in eternal love of God, never to be separate. That is what happens when you get out of the illusion.

You have to become very serious if you are going to make it – very, very serious. The illusion is so powerful, and it is meant to be. To get out of this material existence of non-stop agony, to break out of the prison, to wake up from the dream, to come Home is practically impossible. It is harder to achieve than escaping Alcatraz: just basically speaking, impossible. In a lifetime, only a handful, at the most, make it Home.

At this time there are thousands who are ready. That is why the help has come. God's hands are reaching down to pick people up now. You have to have two hands up. Surrender to God's hands that are reaching for you, to His help, with 100 percent "yes." God is the only power greater than the prison that you are bound by, and when someone is ready, then He comes; and He has come. Grab His hands in sweet, willing surrender.

The path isn't easy, but there is no price too high. As soon as possible, you need to come into a state of willing surrender. It is everything that is waiting for you. It is Home. It is. It's ever-increasing ecstasy. It's eternal life now. And it is peace in His embrace.

I long for you to find your way, to find your way Home. There is a little part inside of you that can remember, but mostly you have forgotten that there is a Home, that there is God, and that it is everything. And in that everything of splendor and glory rests the self in Him. That is where the self is resting.

Once you find your way, then you will be finally and forever free, and you will know where you are. It is not a state you can conjure up. You will know because you will be free. My longing is very great for you to find your way. It is ever-increasing; just as the love is ever-increasing, so is the longing ever-increasing. I long for the people, God's longing, tears of longing. Some people think that God doesn't care, but that is not true. He has sent you so much help. So come. Just trust and come.

# Courage

*Don't let the fear stop you.*

GOURASANA

*Have courage.*
*Courage doesn't mean there's no fear.*
*Courage means you're just*
*brave enough to face the fear.*
*So be courageous on your path*
*and face the fear*
*and go through what you have to*
*go through next.*

KALINDI

# Doubt and Fear

*spoken on March 4, 1996*

There are two states of consciousness that everyone will encounter on the path of transformation, on the path to God. They are part of the path. One of those states of consciousness is fear and the other is doubt.

Both fear and doubt are born of the illusion, but your spiritual journey is *through* the illusion into the light. According to your individual path, you are going to run across different degrees of fear and doubt. Doubt and fear are a natural part of the process and should not be something that you try to do away with, but should be something that you embrace and move through with your awareness as they come up.

One of the very first things that Gourasana said to me was:

> You formed an illusion of who you think you are. This illusion is all you know. It is a strong illusion; even when you perceive it for the illusion it is, it will be very difficult to let go. Too long you have thought

this illusion is who you are. We[1] pray your fear won't stop you.[2]

Don't let the fear stop you: that is one of His basic teachings. The Core[3] came to realize what Gourasana was talking about by going through our transformation and actually facing the fear. We came to understand how critical it was to put up a sign and to have in our conscious minds, "Don't let the fear stop you."

As you are changing, as you are moving forward, as you are breaking illusions, as God's energy starts to touch you, fear will come. Change itself produces fear. Most people become frozen when fear comes instead of just moving through it. But if you can sit with the fear, go into the fear, move with the fear and not become frozen in it, if you can be with the fear, it is a great opportunity, because then you can move through it. Always on the other side of the fear there is more awareness, more light, more truth, more love waiting for you. Then you look back and you will see there was nothing to fear, but yet you were still afraid.

You'll get to the point where you have courage. And courage means not that you're not afraid, but it means that you're not afraid to be afraid, that you'll act despite the fear, that you won't let the fear stop you. So fear will come.

Sometimes, at different points for some of you, the fear will become terror. You will need to face that type of fear and terror within the safety of a deep meditation and in an environment that is supportive for you to face your fear. As you go into the

---

[1] When speaking, Gourasana would sometimes say "We," "Us," and "Our." In these cases, He was referring to Himself along with a vast Heavenly Host of true selves.
[2] Gourasana, *Breaking the Cycle of Birth and Death*, Miracle of Love, 4th Edition, 2007, Quote #39.
[3] The Core is the group of seven people who founded this Mission with Gourasana.

terror in meditation, you may want to surround yourself with a few people that you trust, so you have help as you go through the terror that you are dealing with in your consciousness. You want to move through it. You don't want to be stuck all day frozen in fear. When fear comes, you want to move through it in meditation until you come again to a calm state, and then take whatever action you need to take, make whatever changes you need to.

It may be that you do not have to do anything or take any action; you are simply facing fear. You are just having a feeling of fear, and you just need to be with it in meditation, to release it and open up again. You can always scream into a towel.[4] It doesn't matter how afraid you get. There may even be nothing going on to be afraid of, but you are moving so rapidly internally, and that can feel like fear.

Sometimes when God starts to approach you, the force and power of His energy is very great, and sometimes that energy produces fear as it comes toward you. God's energy is not something to fear; it is just love, but the power of the love is so great that the nervous system and the mind translate the feeling of that much love and energy coming toward you as something to be feared. It is from the mind and the nervous system that the fear is coming; fear is from this illusory plane.

Fear will come and fear will go, and terror will come and terror will go. Some of you won't face so much terror, but some of you will. You really need to embrace the meditation practice.[5] Practice it and learn it, so that you know what to do when fear

---

[4] When Kalindi says "screaming into a towel," she is referring to a spiritual practice often used in meditation, to scream into a towel that you hold over your mouth and vocal cords and release or scream from deep in your gut. This practice is used in Part One of the Modern-Day Meditation in which emotional release takes place.
[5] The Modern-Day Meditation. See Glossary of Names and Terms in the back of the book.

strikes. Learn the meditation so that you can move through the feeling of the fear and then come again to a calm state, where you can then think and move forward with your daily functioning.

If it is that God is trying to move into you, then you can move through the fear, so God can move even more through you. The fear comes because the mind gets in the way; something that seems to be foreign is around you, and you become afraid.

There may be challenges in your life and that brings on fear. You can feel changes coming; you might not even know what the changes are, but you can feel the change coming, and you become afraid. So, fear is something that you want to move through.

Doubt is part of the path. Everyone will have doubts, and it is through your awareness that you will know truth and be able to conquer the doubts. But the doubts are not something that you should beat yourself up about. The doubts also need to be embraced, in a sense, with your awareness. A big part of the path is going to consist of questioning: "What am I doing? What is happening? What is going on? What am I hearing? Is that the truth? Am I moving right?" There will be a lot of questioning; and healthy questioning is very good. A mature seeker will always have healthy questioning going on.

But there is healthy questioning and then there is unhealthy questioning. Healthy questioning means you ask questions from your awareness, and you don't let yourself become swallowed up by doubt. You need to live in your awareness as you are questioning, as you are searching for truth. Questioning is something that is good; it is a natural part of the path. You will come to the truth because you will question. You will question: "What is light? What is dark? What is true? What is not true?" Doubt is a part of the illusion. You want to beware of the doubt. You want to walk through your doubts with your awareness always watching them, with your awareness always talking to you.

I will share with you something that Gourasana spoke to me, and you will come to realize this also as you move spiritually more and more: "Begin to see the power behind the doubt, how great it is. No matter how impressive or great your spiritual experiences have been, there are times where you wonder if any of it is even real."[6] This will happen to you, time and time again. No matter how much light you have experienced, when the doubt comes, you will doubt whether any of the light that you experienced was even real. That is why you have to have your awareness talking to you as you are doubting, because your awareness knows the truth.

If nothing else, when the doubt comes, then appreciate the potency of the illusion. That is what you can do when you doubt. Look at how powerful the illusion is. You have experienced so much light, and now you are working through some layer of illusion or some darkness, and in the midst of that, doubt comes. And when the doubt comes, your mind denies any light that you previously had. So, look at the potency of the illusion and understand that doubt is illusion. Begin to perceive the doubt more and more as part of the illusion. As you practice seeing the doubts, the illusion will begin to weaken, because from an aware state, from your awareness, you will be perceiving the illusion. That is why your awareness is the key, and it needs to be there with you as you walk through your fears and your doubts. With your awareness, you will be able to see that the doubt is just the illusion. You will come to understand these things more and more as you experience directly what doubt does to you.

[6] Gourasana, *Breaking the Cycle of Birth and Death*, Miracle of Love, 4th Edition, 2007, Quote #52.

I think there is a phrase called "demon doubt." It is of the illusion. Doubt is so powerful that when the doubt comes, it completely blinds you to remembering direct truth that you know you have experienced within.

So you have to live from your awareness. Face your fear. When doubt comes, let the doubt be there. Look at it. Watch how covered over it has you, and sit there and say, "Well, I don't even think anything is happening to me spiritually; I have spent three years endeavoring, and nothing has happened." You will see. You will go on and on like this with your doubt. But if you can look at it from your awareness, you can see the illusion and how the illusion is playing with you while you are doubting.

You will do self-questioning. It is a natural part of the process. And as you are questioning whether you can trust the path that you are walking, whether you can trust your teacher, whether you can trust your master, you will have doubt. You have to have your awareness there, speaking truth to you. Otherwise the illusion will get you totally in your doubts. And then the fear will come in, and with the fear and the doubt together, you don't have a chance against the illusion. So you have to live from your awareness.

When you live from your awareness, you will be able to tap into two tools that come to you from the spiritual realm – trust and faith. Trust and faith are so important. They carry you so much of the time. But you also have to be living in your awareness in order to pull from your trust and faith at the same time you are having your doubts. You have to be facing your fear as you are going through your self-questioning, and not be captured by the illusion while you are going through all of that. Trust and faith come to you from God, and you need to live in your awareness in order to conquer the doubts and fears, to move through them, and not let the illusion capture you. Trust and faith – that is the way.

Do not allow the illusion to stop you because of your fear or your doubt. Live in your awareness. Go through your doubts and fears and self-questioning. Go through the terror that some of you may feel. Go through all of it from a conscious, aware state and pull on your trust and faith that come to you from God. As you move through each layer of doubt and each layer of fear, you will come into more direct realization, and you will have more awareness, and that will bring you more trust and faith.

You can't find your way out of the illusion, back to the Lord, back to God out of the illusion without trust and faith. You can't. Without trust and faith, there is no way. And trust and faith come from living in an aware state. The doubts will be there. You can't chase them away. They will be there, but look at them from awareness. The fear will be there; move through it, don't let it stop you. These things are all part of the path.

Practice the Modern-Day Meditation and live it in your daily life. Learn how to live this practice. Do not just use it when you are meditating for a period of time, but live it in your daily life. Living this practice will help you to live in your awareness, so that when doubts and fear come, when it is time that you need to do some questioning, you will be in a calm state in order to receive truth from within. The illusion wants you to be disturbed, because if you are disturbed, then it can capture you. The meditation practice will help you live in awareness, so that you are never stopped by your fear no matter how great it gets, and so that you are never captured by your doubt.

Doubts will come; they will. One of the biggest ways that the illusion bothers you is through doubts. You are going to question. And you need not feel guilty about self-questioning; it is a natural part of the process. But from awareness, you will have the gifts of trust and faith that come from God. As you experience more and more light and more and more love from God, there will be more trust and faith for you to pull on. So again, the Modern-Day Meditation will help you to be able to deal with the fears and the doubts and the self-questioning.

If you want truth, you will find truth. And doubts won't stop you and fear won't stop you and the self-questioning won't stop you. Live in awareness, and pray for more awareness. Don't try to get rid of the fear. Don't try to get rid of the doubts. And don't try to deny yourself the questioning that will go on in your inner search. Just situate yourself in awareness. Practice the Modern-Day Meditation so that you can be in a calm state, so that you can access truth, so that you can access your trust and your faith. Your trust and your faith is what will take you to God. Trust and faith is what will help you when the fear is so great and when the doubts are so consuming. Trust and faith are part of your awareness, and your awareness is directly connected to God. So, live in your awareness.

# Suicide Is Not an Escape

*spoken on October 2, 1997*

These next words that I speak to you are so critical; they are so
important for you to try to hear and understand. Some of it may
be information that you already know, and some of it is information that you do not know. I speak the following words for
everyone on this planet.

There is so much pain, agony, loneliness, despair, distress, heart-
ache, hopelessness, anger, rage, blame, depression, fear; on and
on the list goes, running rampant in this world. If you look, you
will see that this is a fact. How everyone is dealing with it is all
individualized. Some people are dealing with it; some people are
not. Some people are dealing with it more easily than others.
Some people have found a way to deal with it, and some people
have not.

We have young children in this world in so much distress. And of
course, there is so much abuse going on. We have teenagers that
are lost and in despair. In every age bracket, there is suffering going on. This is not to say that there is not some happiness felt here
and there. But if you look around into the eyes of everyone, you

will see what I am speaking of, and this needs to be addressed worldwide. Help needs to start to come worldwide. There are many different ways for people to be helped on their journey in their life, be it a material quest, a spiritual quest, or just the evolution of one's life.

The adults on the planet are suffering, and they are in denial for the most part. The children and the teenagers have nowhere to go to find the truth because of the denial that lives in so many adults. The smiling faces of miserable adults – the children see right through it, and the children suffer from it. And the adults suffer from it, too.

Now there are two things I want to talk to you about. The first thing is that while you walk the face of this earth, you are in a physical body, a human body. It is physical, you can feel it: skin, bones, hair, teeth. You have a physical body. And that is very real to you, and you know that you need to take care of that body for it to function properly. In other words, if you are sick, you know you need to get medication for your body. If you have a fever, you need to take care of yourself. If you have a toothache, you need to go to the dentist. If you break a bone, you need to have it fixed. You don't have any problem taking care of your physical body.

But there is more than just your physical body within your human existence as you walk this earth. You have an emotional body, which needs to be taken care of. You actually have several bodies. I am only going to mention a few. You have your emotional body. You have a psychological body. You have a mental body. You have a spiritual body. Those are a few. And all of these bodies, just like your physical body, need proper attention and care, and you need to identify which body is which, and which body needs what type of care.

There needs to be an opening in people's consciousness to the care of the mental body and the psychological body, which are not the same as the spiritual body and the spiritual movement that happens in one's being. If your mental body carries depression, anxiety, and feelings that you can't go on anymore, no amount of spiritual work will take care of a state of depression. You need to look at your mental and psychological well-being, just like you do your physical well-being.

Don't just wait to think that your spiritual movement, or God, will make your mental well-being be okay. Sometimes that may be the case, but if you have a persistent feeling of just drowning in a depressed state, or a state where you feel like you can't make it one more day, then you need to go to see the type of doctor who takes care of the mental and psychological bodies, and that is not a spiritual teacher. A spiritual teacher, or a spiritual master, or a spiritual path, or a priest, does not take care of your mental, psychological problems; and those problems can be very detrimental, even worse than a physical disease, if they are not seen to by the proper physician.

Some of you may need to go to therapy; you may need to talk to a psychologist. Some of you possibly have chemical imbalances that need attention. Some of you may have so much rage; all of the feelings that I talked about earlier are coming to the surface for you, and you just don't know how you can deal with any of it. You may need to go to an M.D. – a psychiatrist – and tell the doctor what you are experiencing. For a period of time, perhaps, you may need to take some type of medication that balances out your mental and psychological well-being so that you can go on in a healthy state. There is nothing wrong with that. It does not mean that you are crazy if you take a medication prescribed by a doctor that helps you if you are depressed, or you are feeling that you just can't make it: even feeling like going to work every day is just too hard.

There is nothing wrong with taking medication for a period of time until you are stabilized, and that period of time may be a long time. It won't hurt your spiritual movement. I want to really drive that point into all of you, everyone. I don't want everyone to rush off to the psychiatrist and get drugs for your problems. But there are key symptoms that you can feel when you know, "My God, no matter who I talk to, I feel like I am just going on a downward spiral." You need to not be afraid to go to a doctor for your mental and psychological well-being and take medication that is prescribed to you.[1]

What is happening in this day and age is so monumental; the purging of feelings that is going on across the world right now is so big, that you just may need some help to get by for a while. So start to view your mental health and your psychological health the same way you view your physical health. If you have suicidal thoughts, if you sit around thinking about suicide, see a doctor, because that is not a healthy state to live in.

Then you have your spiritual body, which is going through so much also. I want to say at this point that sometimes you move spiritually with the power and energy of God that is coming in so very, very fast. For some of you who are moving fast spiritually – letting go, releasing, opening up to the energy of God – it is going so fast that it tips the scale into the mental area, and it is just too much. All of a sudden, you have reached your limit; you can hardly take any more. You need to understand that it is

---

[1] In this talk, Kalindi is not diagnosing or giving any advice regarding what you need to do to take care of your physical or emotional well-being, other than suggesting that you see the proper professionals in those areas.

not bad to seek the help of a doctor who works in the area of mental problems. The medications prescribed by a doctor for mental problems will not stop your spiritual movement.

I want to get any concept out of the way that it is bad to seek psychiatric help. People may need certain medication at certain times in their lives to help them. You should not fear that. Sometimes it will be for a short period that people need medication, sometimes for a long period, and sometimes on and off. It is not something to fear. Some people just need a psychologist to work out some problems. But don't let yourself slip to a point where you become so hopelessly lost in despair that the only way out that you can think of is suicide.

*Suicide is in no way a way out.* It does not help your situation at all. It is not okay to take your own life. You have a certain destiny to live out, as hard as it may feel or be. There is a lot of help on the planet, and you need to reach out and get that help. You just cannot give up. Suicide is not the answer, even when you are at the end of your rope. I want to scream, "Stop!" You cannot use suicide as an escape to end your suffering. It will not end your suffering.

What will happen, if you choose suicide, is that when you die, you will just be without your current body, but you will have your subtle body, which is another body. And in that subtle body will be your consciousness that you died with. You will be stuck in a very dark place, facing the very things that you could not stand to face while you had a body. Only it will be more difficult, because you won't be able to do anything about it except sit there and look at it, twenty-four hours a day, for a long time, maybe up to sixty years.

Suicide is one of the worst deaths to have. It keeps you on the other planes after death longer than almost any other type of death, before taking birth again. It keeps you longer than practically anything else. And you are just sitting there staring at what you couldn't stand to face.

So you don't get free from any of your problems by shooting yourself, by killing yourself in some way, whatever way you do it. You don't get rid of the pain and the suffering. Killing yourself will not do it. If you do this, then you face what you could not stand while you were alive until you come to a point where you are ready to come back again; then you pick up where you left off, and you have to do it again.

So for those of you who think suicide is a way out, you are sadly mistaken. It gets worse if you commit suicide. Now there is no eternal hell, but it gets pretty bad for quite a while facing a black pit of despair. The same black pit that you chose to commit suicide over becomes even blacker when you do not have a body, or any help, or a way to deal with your problems; there is just you, sitting there, facing it. And you have to face it for a long time, as I said, up to as much as sixty years, and then you take birth again. Then you face it some more until you get through it.

*Suicide is not okay.* Sometimes when someone commits suicide, people say, "Well, at least their suffering is over." Stop saying that, because that is a lie. Their suffering is not over. Feel compassion for that being, and pray for that being. But their suffering is not over by any means. They still have to face everything, and more.

There is so much to face in between births until you break free. Again, I will tell you, *suicide is one of the worst things to do because you stop your destiny.* You don't play it out. You don't go to the end. No matter how horrible what you have to face is, you have to play it out while you are alive. You have to get through it, and then you take birth again, and you can continue. But if you commit suicide, you stop, and you have to face it all while you are out there without a body, just in your subtle body. And it is very uncomfortable.

Now I want to know who in this world is willing to transform and face themselves, and find truth, find love, and find God to a point where they can turn around and be of service to this suffering world – a world of very little love, where there are so many people wanting to commit suicide, so many people suffering in so many ways?

Every different type of suffering is going on here. Who will stop living for their own selfish life and turn the corner and come toward the light into transformation so that the people of this world can be helped? Because the people of this world are crying for help – children, teenagers, adults, and older people are crying for help. Now who is going to offer that help?

I know there are a lot of people who are trying their best to help. There is a lot of help available, but not enough. And the help needs to become purer and purer, which means the love of God has to enter. How does the love of God enter? It comes from serious spiritual transformation.

So I urge you – those of you who will transform – transform. And, I say again, *suicide is no way out of your pain in any way.* Everything becomes worse. You don't escape anything.

Please reach out somewhere, to someone, if you feel bad. If you have these feelings, take care of your mental and psychological body and go see a doctor. There is nothing wrong with that. It does not mean you are crazy. It does not mean you are insane. There is a big transformation going on worldwide, and you might be stuck in the middle of it and just don't know what to do. You just may need to see a doctor who can help you mentally, so that you can stand up and exist in this world, which is not an easy thing to do. It is not. It is very hard to survive in this world, very hard. It is not easy, and a lot of times it feels like there is just no purpose for it. "Why stand up, why be strong, why even live?" That goes on in so many people's minds. But you must, and you must seek the help that you need.

So start watching out for each other, and start watching out for yourself. And as hopeless as it seems, there is so much hope. God is here with so much help for you. Those of you who say you don't believe in God, I say to you: you do believe in God. Because when tragedy strikes, the words that come out of your mouth are, "Oh, my God." *You do believe in God, and it is God that will help.*

And it will take all responsibility from you to act in a proper way in every situation in your life, no matter what age you are. As a small child, you are very dependent on your parents. So those of you who are parents, you need to take a lot of responsibility into your hands. You need to learn how to be open with your children. Understand them. Try to understand them. They are living in a time that is very difficult, different than the difficulties of the past. They are living in a time of transformation where there is a lot of confusion and upheaval. So try to have some understanding for what is going on.

I don't want to go on and on much longer about this; I just want people to get it. Go to the doctor, reach out to support groups, and know that *suicide is not ever a solution, never, ever.*

If you are dying, and you are using some kind of life support, something is being used to keep you alive and if it were not used, nature would take you – that is not suicide. To let nature take you because God is calling you, is not suicide. It is a natural death. But anything other than that is not living out what you need to live out; you are going to have to face it.

I speak a lot now about suicide; not just for older people, but I speak a lot for the young ones, the teenagers, the young adults. And I ask the older, mature adults: please, please, wake up. Open your eyes. And I ask the young adults: start to come together with each other. Know what is going on with each other. Help each other. Suicide is not okay. And taking medication to help you get through certain periods of your life is fine. There is nothing wrong with that.

# Determination

*Your job is to never give up.*

GOURASANA

*The illusion doesn't fall away overnight.*
*It takes time and steady work and serious desire.*
*And it takes seekers with fiber with intense*
*desire and dedication and commitment*
*to walk through the fire of spiritual transformation*
*to actually achieve self realization.*
*It doesn't come easy. It is completely possible.*
*There's so much assistance from God.*
*There's so much guidance, there's so much*
*power available directly from the Source.*
*But it doesn't come easy. It's not easy*
*by any means – the path to self-realization.*

KALINDI

# Never Give Up

*spoken on March 12, 1995*

For every one of you, probably the most important phrase in your life is "Never give up." You will all need to remember, at different points in your life and in your transformation, to never give up and to have trust and faith in God. *Never give up, and have trust and faith in God.*

Everyone is going to cross through a lot in transformation. It is not a bad thing – the transformation. It is not a negative thing, even though there is sometimes great pain and fear. It is not negative; it is not bad. You are actually going for the greatest achievement possible.

You are going through something that at times is very difficult and trying, and sometimes you don't know what is happening.

You have to have trust and faith during those times. Sometimes you get very afraid; there is too much pain, and you don't want to do it anymore. At those times, you have to put a big sign up on your wall that says, "Never Give Up." And then every night before you go to sleep during this period, when you have made it through another day, you can put a check mark on your Never Give Up sign.

To become free of the attachment that has you bound in all areas is no small feat, no easy task. And that is what you are asking for – to become free of all of your attachments to the illusion, so that you can live in a state of freedom inside of yourself. That is a place of total openness and no denial, in union with God.

So you may be hearing this phrase for a long time. Don't say four years from now, "It has been four years. How many more times, Kalindi, are you going to tell me not to give up?" Well, I'm going to tell you not to give up until you have succeeded. And you need to get ready for the long haul. What is four years? What is ten years really, if you achieve ultimate freedom?

So all you need to concern yourself with is that you are doing everything you can do, every single day, to become closer to God, more surrendered to God, and more giving in the service of God. Every day, watch yourself achieve more awareness, more consciousness, and become freer and freer.

Let the times that are difficult come, and welcome those times. You can be afraid of those times, but don't stop what you need to feel in the midst of that great movement that is going on.

One of the main reasons that I am here is to give you faith to not give up, and to let you know, "Yes, you're going through that. Yes, it's hard. Yes, there's fear. Yes, there's pain. Yes, yes, yes, that is the way it is. Do it, and don't give up!" I want to bring you whatever faith, encouragement, guidance, love, and energy I can bring to you. *Don't give up.*

Remember those words at the time when you are ready to give up, and you are thinking, "That's it. I can't take it anymore. How much further is there? How much deeper is there? How much darker is it? How much thicker is it? When exactly am I going to get free? Is there such a thing as freedom? Is there even a God? What am I doing, anyway? What, am I crazy? What is this that I do in my life, confronting myself, lying on the floor screaming,[1] spending hours letting go with desire?"

If there were another way to go through transformation that I knew about, I would let you know. But one thing I know is that the way I am guiding you, you will succeed if you get on your hiking boots and go through the swamps like a brave soldier with courage. Courage means that you are not afraid to be afraid. It doesn't mean there is no fear. It means despite the fear, you will be brave and go forward and do what you need to do – whatever that is – to break you free in the next situation, in the next area in your life. It means you are not afraid to make the changes, you are not afraid to feel the pain, you are not afraid to be afraid. Everybody is afraid to be afraid and everybody is afraid of the pain. So you need to become courageous and never give up. Just never, ever, ever, give up.

Don't let the fear stop you. Don't let your judgments, concepts, and beliefs stop you. Find whatever is going on inside of you that is holding you back. Is it fear? Is it judgment? Is it a concept? Is it a belief? You need to dislodge yourself from those things so you can keep moving forward. I can tell you, a lot of times it makes no sense what is happening to you next. It is the last thing you

---

[1] When Kalindi says, "lying on the floor," she is referring to meditating using the Modern-Day Meditation; it is common to start the meditation practice by sitting on the floor. When Kalindi says "screaming," she is referring to a spiritual practice often used in meditation to help with opening the emotional body: hold a towel over your mouth and vocal cords and release or scream from deep in your gut.

want to go through. It is the last thing you think you should be feeling. It is the last thing you wanted to face. And it is right up against you. What are you going to do?

So how much will you do between this month and next month to move yourself forward – in your connection to God, in your awareness, in your heart, and in the material foundation that is supporting you in this world? How much will you get through this month? Will you take your meditations seriously?

You have to meditate. You have to, because it is the only way God can get in and talk to you – even though you can't stand it, really. You need to sit there long enough to become open to a place where true hearing is happening. If you want the truth, you have to meditate. You have to go within very deeply, and you have to be open. You have to open up your whole being so God can get to you. So if for some reason you can't come to the Center on a certain night,[2] it's okay. But then make sure you meditate at home at least twice a week for a couple of hours. Take a half an hour or an hour on the other days to sit down and go within, ask, and seriously endeavor to find the truth of what you need to do next in whatever area you are confronting.

If you want to find the truth and not be cheated or sidetracked or swayed by the illusion, then you will see to it that you are going within and acting upon the truth that is coming to you – not acting on something coming from your mind that is in response to a fear you have, or making a decision based on a judgment. You will see that in a very clear, open state, you are finding the answers that you need to help you on your way. It takes a lot of sincerity on your part.

---

[2] Group meditations are held several times a week at Path Centers worldwide.

So never give up. And as this month goes by, double your efforts. Don't settle for just another month going by. How far can you go this month? You have mountains to move, so push over a few hills this month. You all know what you are up against individually. Will you become determined enough to break through the next area that you are up against? Determination.

Your hours of prayer are not going unheard. Your hours of prayer are being answered. You don't necessarily like the answer that you get all the time, but you are being heard. So keep going through whatever is coming up next; just keep going.

I can tell you right now, it is the same thing for everyone. When the going gets tough, everyone wants to give up. That is how it is when it gets really bad for everyone. That is how it was for me, that is how it was for The Lady, that is how it was for Jim, that is how it was for my whole Core.[3] It is a natural feeling; don't worry about it. When you want to give up, all you have to do is know that, "Well, I'm not giving up. I feel like giving up. I can't take it anymore. But I'm not giving up, because I'm never going to give up. Never. I'm going to succeed!"

Knowing that you will never give up and that you are going to succeed will carry you through whatever you have to go through. Knowing this will allow you to feel some ecstasy and some joy about what is actually happening to you, despite how bad it might feel at times. Let some joy and ecstasy come, because you are going to succeed as long as you don't give up.

Some of you may have to move to a different path or process or do something different along the way. That is fine. Just do

---

[3] The Core is the group of seven people who founded this Mission with Gourasana.

whatever you need to do on your path. Just don't give up. *Just don't give up.* And if you have to move over here or over there, don't give up. My energy and my love are with you. Just hear my voice: "Don't give up."

No matter where you are in your life, God is following you around. No matter what you have to do, don't give up in your quest for God. Don't ever think, "I've been gone for so long. I've gotten so much, but it always goes away. I get it and it goes. I get it and it goes. I don't believe in it anymore, because it never stays." You just have to keep going. God takes you through everything.

You can count on the fact that whatever is inside of you, you are going to face it. No stone will go unturned. You can picture yourself as this little light being that is buried underneath a pile of gravel, and every pebble of the pile of gravel has to go. Some of those pebbles you are very attached to, and you think that they belong to you or that they have something to do with you. When that pebble starts to get moved by God, you get disturbed, sometimes to a point of wanting to give up: "I'm not going to do this." Do it anyway. Don't give up. Come bursting through all the pebbles of gravel until you are flying in who you are – just flying in who you are. You will know when you are with God, when you are truly with God. You will be totally at peace and at one with God.

One who wants God will not stop short or be fooled by any experience, by any state, by anything. You can let all the states and experiences come and go, and you can experience joy and laughter and ecstasy. But for someone who is sincere, you will keep on going until you have found your way Home. When you find your way Home, you know you are Home. You don't have to tell anyone, and you don't have to try to figure out if it is true. When you are Home, you are Home.

Never give up. Work hard this month. It is solely up to you.

Some people think that God doesn't care – that we pray, we pray, we pray, we pray, and God doesn't hear. But that is not what is going on. That is not the reason why results are not happening. God cares so much. I know the care that God has and how much desire God has for you. If you can just have as much desire for God as God has for you, then your path will go at lightning speed. God cares. And God is sending everything to you to help you. He cares, and He wants to give you the eternal love and the ecstasy that your heart longs for. God wants to give you the eternal relationship with the Divine that your soul longs for. You just have to want that, too. And you have to let go of all of your concepts along the way so that you can have all of God.

When you come to the times where you have had it – not just when you are frustrated about the little stuff, but when you start crashing into intense areas of movement – all you need to do is go into the feeling and release the fear. Go into the pain to a depth where you can release and calm down. Then in a calm state, all you need to do is ask, "What do I need to do next? What is the very next thing I need to do?" You don't need to be thinking about anything else. You don't need to be thinking about one week from now or one month from now or what your life is going to be like or, "Oh, my God." No! You need to calm all the way down to where you are just thinking about one thing, and that is, "What do I need to do right now? What is the very next step for me?" Because once you take that step, then you will be able to go on to the next thing. While you are frozen in fear and are avoiding feeling the pain, there is no way you can find out what the next step is. First, you have got to go within and open up and feel the feelings.

If you are trying to find out what to do based on a state of up-heaval, don't waste your time, because you won't find the right answer. You have got to first open up, release, and then calm down and then ask, "What do I need to do next?" It's very simple.

Sometimes all you can do is go day by day asking, "What is the very next thing I need to do?"... "Oh, in two weeks I need to move." So that would be something that you would need to start to think about. If you have to move out of your house in two weeks, then I would imagine that is something that you would need to focus on totally. It doesn't matter if you are afraid what might happen two weeks from now. If, all of a sudden, you sold your house today and you have to move in two weeks, then it is really clear what you have to focus on. The fear that you have in the rest of your life doesn't really matter at the moment.

Do you understand? Get through whatever the fear is. Get a grip. And focus on what is next. You might have to think even more specifically about something. For example, if you have to move in two weeks, you might think, "What do I have to do tomorrow about that?" Or, "I lost my job today and I'm going to be out of money in a month." So, rather than going into total fear and panic – which you may be in – go deeper into the fear and panic, move the feeling, open up, release, calm down, and think from an open state. You will find answers and guidance inside that will take you to the next place.

Maybe it is easy for you to hear me now, and it sounds very logical when you are calm. But when everything is tipped over, you forget about this. So try to remember to move the feelings.

Go into them. Open up. Release. Then calm down. If you can't calm down to a very sane, sober place where you can make a decision based on clarity – instead of fear and judgment – then you haven't released what you have to release in order to find the answer you are looking for. You have to be able to calm down. You can't calm down a state of fear that is frozen; it has to open up. If you try to calm down your fear, then you will just be sitting there calm in your fear looking for answers based upon fear.

Support each other when you come to these kinds of places; help each other to stop, just stop. Help each other, either to go into the feelings and get calm or to decide to not think about anything right now until you can release and calm down. Don't let each other just run around, spinning around. Help each other to go within and open up so you can get to some accurate decisions. Help each other and watch out for each other and be there for each other.

For some of you, your transformation is going to be easier in a lot of ways than for others. If it's easier for you, if hardly anything bothers you, if you are one who can take anything, you are going to come to some really hard spots. Those hard spots will be from deep inside that have nothing to do with anything in the world, or any kind of fear that you have about anything in the world. You are going to be up against very deep issues inside that will be difficult for you. So you will have your own times where you hit hard spots. You are just going to face it, and you will have the strength to go through it.

Everyone will hit up against everything. So do it with some joy – because you are coming Home, because you are finding your way to the freedom that you are asking for. Don't do it thinking that your transformation is a "bummer." It is not a bummer. It is everything that you have ever wanted. Have some joy about that. Have some gratitude in your life that it is happening to you. Put some dance music on, at least once a day, even if you are afraid. Help each other, okay?

# Break Out – Break Free

*spoken on March 3, 1996*

I want to somehow reach part of your consciousness that can hear the following words. I have several points to make, and it is vital that you grasp all of them in order for you to understand the transformation that you are going through – and will be going through – if you are going to break free from the illusion. I am speaking these words to you, not to have you feel hopeless by the end of this talk, but to give you hope by giving you some explanation.

An understanding of the illusion needs to come into your awareness. The illusion is the force that separates you from yourself, from God, from truth, from love. This understanding comes in gradual increments. I understand you don't have any idea how to break out of the illusion, how that is going to happen. I understand your predicament, because I also sat in the same predicament. I didn't understand, and I was given some basic, simple words of guidance. I was blessed to have Gourasana as my spiritual master, and He brought forth very simple words; He did not speak a lot of words, but I listened. I wanted to break free so badly. I knew that this material world at its best was still suffering, and I wanted to find my way Home.

One thing that Gourasana had me focus on for a long time is the illusion and how the illusion works. It works to trap you. It works to bring you just enough light to suck you in, to allure you into its web. Then you suffer. And it does this repeatedly to you. But because you don't know anything else, because you have forgotten that there is freedom, forgotten that there is God, forgotten that there is your true self, you fall prey to the traps of the illusion over and over again.

The reality is that to be caught in the material world is to be in prison. And anything that appears to be happiness is nothing more than a decoration in your prison cell. One way the illusion, the prison, keeps you bound and trapped is by keeping you unaware of its workings.

This illusion, this prison that you are in, is guarded by a jailhouse warden, who knows exactly what to do to trick you and trap you over and over again. It is such an insidious force. It is meant to be that way. And its purpose is to keep you in separation. It works day and night against you.

When you start to find light, the illusion is right there to grab at you and take you, with that light, and just turn you a little bit the other way. So you fall right back into the trap of the prison, but with a better decorated cell. Then you think you are happy. And as soon as you fall for the trap, it is just a matter of time before suffering comes again. Even when you are happy, there is suffering. But everyone has forgotten that there is something else outside of this illusion.

If you want to break free, you have to get very wise to the warden's tricks. And you have to get very aware of your weaknesses and to how you fall prey to the jailhouse warden, who knows exactly how to trap you. All that needs to happen is that you get trapped just enough so you don't make it Home in this lifetime. And then you take birth again (whether you believe that or not). You don't get out of material consciousness, out of the material world, until you break out, break free. You have to break out of the prison.

One thing that no one wants to face is the fact that every single person in this prison called "the material world of illusion" is sentenced to death. You are all on execution row. That is the nature of this prison. That is one thing you can count on for sure: you will meet your death. It will be either a short death or a long death – perhaps a horrible death, perhaps a short horrible death, perhaps a long horrible death. But you don't die at the death of the body; you continue on, and you continue on in prison according to where your consciousness is trapped at the time of your death.

The only way out is to wake up to the fact that you are indeed in prison, guarded by an illusory force, a jailhouse warden that knows every different way to keep you trapped. The warden knows how to make you be able to receive so much light that you are completely fooled, believing that the light that you have is full and complete. It is so insidious. The illusion goes right along with you, as you are moving toward the light, and at every step of the way, it disguises itself to fool you. "Oh, come over this way!" And you fall for it again.

For you to break out of the prison, you have to have the specific desire to break out. You are not sentenced to prison for eternity with a repeated death sentence over and over again. You are here in the illusion, bound by the illusion, until you are ready to break free of the illusion. Once you are ready to break free, once you want God fully, then you will take the necessary steps; you will do what you need to do to wake up your consciousness. You will understand that you are sentenced to death and that you do not know when that death is going to happen and in what fashion it will come to you.

Once you wake up and once you desire to break free and start to realize that you want God, that you no longer are satisfied with the small amounts of pleasure derived from material consciousness – once you want Him, He answers your prayer. The illusion is not an all-powerful force that has you trapped forever, but it has you trapped until you want God 100 percent. It is only when you want God with that much desire that a power comes to you – God Himself with His mighty force – and helps you break out, break free of the prison of the illusion.

God is the only one who can outsmart the prison warden. When God sends a spiritual master to assist you to break free, the master brings different words of truth and different types of assistance to help you in your battle to break free from the illusion. Once you want out of the illusion and your intent is to do whatever it takes to break out, God will bring you all the power, all the assistance, all of the guidance that you need in order to see the illusion clearly and to fully awaken your awareness so that you can start to shed the illusion, and so that your true self can begin to manifest.

God's power is great. God is great. And God is more powerful than the illusion. But you have to get on God's side totally. You have to use all parts of your being – your intelligence, your mind, your body, your energy – to break free. Every part of you needs to be used to help God in assisting you to break out. If you are fighting God, He is not going to force you. He has given you free will to play in this illusory world. He has given you free will to try to find happiness in this prison for as long as you like. He will not interfere with that. He will only help you as you really, truly want to be helped, which means you have to help yourself as He is helping you.

I want to bring you some hope. God is bringing in a power that is so mighty that it will help you to break free. But you have to be willing to give up the entire illusion. And the illusion falls away bit by bit by bit, chunk by chunk by chunk. It is not just that one day, you are free from illusion. It is a process of transformation, and you have to give your life to it. And you can't waste any time.

I'm not only telling you there is God; there is also an energy that comes from God. I'm trying to somehow let you know that there is a special energy, a special assistance, that knows the prison warden very well. And if you will practice the Modern-Day Meditation, you can open up to that special assistance. When you do this meditation, this special assistance can enter you with transformational energy; this energy helps you open up so that you can heal, so that you can break free, so that your true self can begin to manifest. The special assistance will bring you awareness you need in order to succeed. The meditation practice is vital for you to be able to see the illusion, and see how it traps you, and see how it tricks you.

You have to be aware constantly. You have to live always in a conscious state of awareness, always wanting the highest truth. You have to snap awake. If you want to break free, you have to snap awake into your spiritual quest and you have to walk straight. You have to walk straight, and you have to go deep within, asking for truth. In your quest, you have to want to hear the truth and want to take action so that you can break out.

As you tap in to God's special assistance to break you free, the transformation process is a bit of a bumpy ride. As He is pulling you out of quicksand, as He is breaking you free out of the prison, as you are chipping away the illusion, as you are going through layer after layer of illusion and through darkness – sometimes hardly being able to see any light – it is a little bumpy. But if you have the intention to break out, if you are on God's side, and you are willing to take action, God will bring you assistance. As your mind becomes your friend and your intelligence is on the side of your true self, and you really want to break free, you will be given information through your meditation practice on what to do next on your journey out of the illusion.

So it is not hopeless at all. There is so much hope. You can break free if you want to, but you have to do your part. You have to have the intent to do it, and you need to get to the point where you have that intent twenty-four hours a day. That doesn't mean that you are not responsible in your life, because part of breaking free from the illusion is that you have things work in your life to support your spiritual quest. The illusion would love to throw your life off balance, so then you can't focus on what you need to do to break free. The illusion would love to have you not be able to work out things in your material life, because then you will be distracted.

The illusion works in many ways. All parts of you have to be lined up and focused on "What do I need to do next, God?" and "I am going to do it as soon as I hear what I need to do. I meditate, listen, go within, find the correct answers, and take the right steps forward toward God, toward truth." You don't do these things to create a better illusion with more of God and God's love. You do these things to walk into total truth.

This transformation is about the annihilation of the ego, the false self. It is very bumpy many times. You need to use your meditation practice. That word "practice" is a good word for you to come to understand; you have to *practice* it. One of the most wonderful gifts that the meditation will bring you is an ability to be open, to allow God's energy – God's transformational power – to enter you, to start to move you through the illusion. And it will help you to also be able to have a calm composure about you, so that you can access the thinking that you need, so you can get solutions and answers, so you can move forward.

Transformation is about moving forward. It is about growth and evolution. It's about getting wise to the tricks of the illusion and day-by-day breaking out more and more.

You need to know that if you don't want to break out, God won't force you, nor can He help you. It is based upon your desire. You have to take the necessary next steps, and you have to move forward as you hear what you need to do, or the illusion will have you wallowing in endless issues. You need to take action and move forward. Your intent has to be "I am going to break free in this lifetime." Your prayer to God has to be so serious. I want to tell you that He will answer you. He will. And as He answers you, you need to embrace the understanding that He is taking you through the illusion, as bumpy as it gets.

One of the biggest things you can do to help yourself is to become a giver. Become a vessel of giving and helping others. That will help you through the bumpy times. Giving brings half of the light coming to you that is moving you through the illusion.

You have to be so strong in your mind. His power is a mighty force. It will set you free, but you have to do your part. You have to have the intent to let go, and then you have to move forward. There are so many of you that are ready for this.

As you pray to God to help you, as you meditate, as you go within for answers, as you go within to open up for healing, have the full intention of "I am going within because I want to let go, and when I hear what to do and when I know what to do, I am going to take steps forward to break the bondage that the illusion has me in." If you can live your life like that, day by day you will break freer and freer of the illusion. You will. God is here to help you, but you have to want it. And you have to help yourself.

The same power from God that has taken me Home – and it is a mighty power – is here for everyone, for whoever wants out of the illusion. You can break out now, but you have to want to break out. And you have to take the steps that you need to take to get out.

I would suggest that you read *Breaking the Cycle of Birth and Death*[1] by Gourasana. Every day, read one page of that and contemplate it. There is so much information in this book, even though the words are simple. I had so much desire; I just needed those simple words. I also needed to open up to His power. With those two things – His guidance, and His power and special assistance – God took me out of the illusion and took me Home, into Him. So now I can help all of you. I was not blessed with some kind of benediction or power from God that is not available to you too.

I am here to give you hope and to point you in the direction of the special assistance of God. It is more powerful than the illusion,

---

[1] Gourasana, *Breaking the Cycle of Birth and Death*, Miracle of Love, 4th Edition, 2007.

and it knows the tricks of the prison warden. And it will assist you in uncovering your true self. With your intent to say "yes" to being with God, with His assistance helping you, and my helping you and acting as a link to that assistance and to that guidance, little by little the illusion will go and you will achieve more and more awareness.

It can happen for you, but you have to want it. You have to recognize that you are in a prison and it will always be a prison, no matter how good it gets. Do you want to be in a pretty prison or do you want to be set free? What does your soul want?

I don't want to steer you in any wrong direction. I will tell you right off the bat that in spiritual transformation to freedom, to break out of the illusion back to the kingdom of God, you will walk through the fire of spiritual transformation. And that fire will burn up the illusion completely, and you will stand in the love and the light and the truth of God. But you have to be willing to walk through that transformational fire. And you have to have great consciousness so that you can make the necessary decisions, so that you can balance yourself as you walk through that fire, so that you can tolerate it, so that you can go the next step. Breaking free is about full awareness; it's about full consciousness. You can't get around anything.

I want you to have hope from this talk. I don't want you to feel hopelessness, or feel like there is no way out. There is a way out; there is. Take a look at your desire and your willingness and what your intention is. Is your intent to let go? Or is your intent to hang on and just have a better life? Or do you want real freedom?

# It's Solely Up to You

*spoken on March 12, 1995*

The thing I want to talk to you about is that your spiritual success or failure is solely your responsibility. It is solely your responsibility whether or not you succeed in your spiritual endeavor toward freedom, toward union with God, toward the love of God, toward becoming freer and freer every day, to have more truth, to break the cycle of birth and death, to go Home in this lifetime, to become a vesselof God's love – whatever it is that you are shooting for.

All of the power, presence, energy, love, and all of the knowledge that you need is pouring in from God at this time to help you to succeed spiritually. If you don't do the necessary work on yourself on the path of transformation – despite your fear, despite your pain, despite whatever you are angry about – you will not succeed; and it will be your own fault. It will not be the fault of the people that were trying to help you, or the spiritual master that you found that was trying to help you, or the Incarnation that was bringing in the power to help you. It will be your fault if you don't succeed spiritually. There is zero reason for anyone not to succeed.

Now the question is, will you have the desire? Will you have the determination? Will you give up your judgments, your concepts, and your beliefs? Will you do what is needed to break through the illusion that separates you from your self and God?

If you want to find your real self, you will have to let go of everything that you think you are. You will have to let go of all attachment. Everything that you are hanging on to is somehow going to get moved out of the way so that you can uncover who you really are.

Nothing will be missing in your life. When you look at letting go of all the attachments from where you are right now, it looks like everything is going to be missing. Everything that you can see, touch, feel, hang on to, and comprehend is all being challenged and moved around. You are afraid that if you let go, you are going to lose something or miss something, but the reality is that everything that you are hanging on to is keeping you separate from being who you are in God. In a state of detachment, your true love can come forth, your true passion can come alive, your true self can live its life. Your true self lives complete in itself with God and is not dependent on anything to make it whole or alive. Your true self doesn't need to strive to have the love of God. It already has it, lives in it, is it. Everything that everyone is hanging on to is blocking that true self from fully living in God's truth and love.

The responsibility of your transformation is yours. Everything that you need is available to you for you to succeed. What do you think about that? The job is up to you. Will you do it? Who exactly are you going to blame this time if you don't succeed? There is a transformation to go through on every level, to bring body, mind, heart, and spirit together to achieve union with God. There is a transformation to go through to bring God all the way inside of you, to set yourself all the way free. You have a lot of work to do on yourself, on many levels.

You have a lot of awareness to develop so that you can find the truth within and not become trapped by the many ways that the illusion tries to trap you. There are many different fancy "gift-wrapped packages" that the illusion wants to lure you with. The more open you get, the more you will enjoy those packages, and there is nothing wrong with enjoying what there is in this world to be enjoyed. There is everything wrong, however, with being lured into attachment by the gifts of this world; you cannot think that anything temporary will bring you your soul's happiness. That is a big mistake. No matter what you can get, no matter what you can achieve materially in this world, no matter how great it is, you will not be satisfied in your heart of hearts.

There is nothing wrong with having the gifts of this world. There is nothing wrong with having them in abundance. And there is nothing wrong with enjoying them fully. In fact, the more open you get when things come your way, the more you can really feel the pleasure because your senses are wide open. You can get maximum enjoyment from the gifts because there is no attachment, and you can really allow yourself to have it all in the moment. There is a big problem if you start letting yourself be trapped by thinking, "This is what is going to make me happy. I have finally found the love I was looking for." If you are basing your happiness and your love and your passion on anything temporary, you will lose it. And you will at some point see that you did not quite have what your soul was searching for.

To find everything that you want, you have a great endeavor to embark upon. And the endeavor is your responsibility. If you take the responsibility, you will start to feel the joy and the ecstasy of the possibility that you are actually going to succeed, because you can feel yourself doing it, not waiting for someone else to do it for you. Take the help, the energy, the assistance, and the guidance available to you; but you need to do the work.

You start to feel inside of you that you are going to reach the greatest achievement humanly possible. You start to know it inside of yourself, even though there are hard spots that you hit. When you take the responsibility and start to feel, "I am going to succeed. I am going to do whatever I have to do. It is going to be all up to me. I know that everything is there for me. I am going to do it," you will simultaneously feel the reality of what is happening to you and that you are going to make it. You will feel happy to surrender, because you will know that you are the one who is letting go, you are the one who is surrendering, and that you are doing it because you want to. And you are doing it because that is what you have to do in order to succeed. You won't be walking around mad at the world for years, mad at every organization that ever existed, mad at every teacher that ever tried to help, mad at every spiritual master that ever tried to bring any teaching to the world.

A spiritual master always tries to bring forth the truth as well as it can be done at the time. There is an awareness about spiritual masters and spiritual truth that needs to emerge now for people; it is solely up to you to find this. There has been a lot of fancy talk in the New Age that there is no need for spiritual masters anymore, that spiritual masters are a thing of the past, that everyone has to find their own power within, and on and on. I am telling you what the truth really is. There is a great need for spiritual masters. The time of the spiritual master is not over. But clarification of what a spiritual master is, is needed. A spiritual master is not someone to be worshipped. They are not people

who are better than you. They are not people who have something more than you or have something that you can never
achieve. The concepts and beliefs that people have had about
spiritual masters need to go. The concepts that people have had
about God, Incarnations, spiritual masters, God Himself, have to
go in order for people to find the truth about spiritual masters.

People have held spiritual masters up on a pedestal, in a place of
worship, in a place of "better than." And they have held God in
the same place, and so it has never quite been possible for people
to find their true power. In order for you to really find your true
power, you will need to find God. You will have no problem
being in a total state of surrender and humility in God, because
that is who you truly are.

A spiritual master or an Incarnation that comes at a current time
carries not only teachings for that time, but an energy, a fragrance
of the Divine. There is a very sweet feeling with the spiritual master or Incarnation so that you can be inspired and encouraged
by the love of God. A rose, when it is fresh, carries a fragrance,
and as it starts to die physically, it is still a rose; it still carries
a certain fragrance. The rose is still what it was, but it is not
carrying the power and the freshness that it did when it was alive.
All of the spiritual masters and Incarnations have come in with
a divine fragrance, and as the years have passed, their existence
and their energy is still felt, but the fragrance and the energy that
they brought starts to wane. That doesn't mean that they were
not who they were and that you cannot still get benefit from your
connection with them.

When there is a current-day spiritual master or Incarnation who
has come, you want to take advantage of that opportunity. You
want to take full advantage of a spiritual master – if you find

yourself sitting with a true master. You will have to search your heart and find out if you have indeed found that for yourself, if the teachings that are being spoken by that spiritual master resonate in your heart. If so, you need to let yourself be fully open to receive the gifts that come from that current manifestation.

There are gifts from God that are here; they are plentiful, and they are pouring in to help you, to guide you, to assist you. But you have to be open to hearing and then moving with the help and the tools that are being given to you. If you don't do it, who are you going to blame? You can't blame the organization or the spiritual master anymore. That is not whose problem it is. This problem that is going on is your problem. It is up to you to find your way. All help is being brought forth to help you, but you have to find your way. You have to let go of putting the responsibility on anyone outside of yourself. A spiritual master can be sitting in front of you; even God Himself can be sitting in front of you, beating on you with a bat to wake you up, and this will do nothing unless you are willing to do the inner work, go within, and let go.

If people do not open to taking the help the way God is bringing it to them, it is going to be a sad situation, because people just are not going to make it Home to God without the help. There needs to be so much help. There is so much illusion and darkness going on. The fear that everyone has of losing their power, or giving everything up, or not having something, has to be worked through. There needs to be an openness to the help that is coming for people.

You must be forever open-minded in your quest for God. At no point in your spiritual transformation can you become locked into a certain way that it needs to feel, needs to look, needs to be. At no point can you become locked in your consciousness, because the very expression of God is going to come in many ways and many flavors and many different experiences. You have no idea how big and ever-expansive God is.

Work hard to let go and have your connections start to come more and more with God. And what you need to do is just let the connections come and let them go, and don't try to have it be just like it was yesterday. Don't try to duplicate it. Don't think, "Why was I so deep last week? I want to go back there again. This person is going really deep; I never do it like that. I have to do it like that!" Don't judge yourself or compare yourself to anyone else's path. Let your path be your path. Again, it is up to your endeavor and your sincerity whether or not you will truly succeed in finding God.

If you are not doing everything that you need to do in your life every day in order to succeed, who is going to lose out but you? Who are you cheating but yourself? If you are not doing your meditation work that you need to do in order to find your connection, who are you trying to fool? If you are trying to tell somebody, "Well, I meditate, and I'm doing this and I'm doing that," but you are not really going to the depths that you need to go to find your connection with God, whose fault is it?

So you need to be very open-minded with your experience of God so that you can experience God in the many ways that God wants to give to you. The ways that God wants to give to you are forever changing and forever expanding. God's love is very glorious. It is love and ecstasy beyond your comprehension. Your judgments, concepts, and beliefs need to go so that you can start to move in God's flow. You cannot be on some trip with your connection to God. You cannot be trying to prove to other people, "Look at me and what I have," because you won't have it when you are trying to prove it. You will have lost the real connection. Again, you need to be openminded; let it come, let it move, and if you are not doing what you need to do, then you are going to sit in your own mess, because there is no reason for you to not make it to God. Not if you want to.

You need to be so open-minded. When you are with God, there is nothing but open-mindedness. That is why you can accept every different flavor of God that comes your way and every different way; and He is many different ways. He. It. Don't be hung up when I say "He," those of you that want to say "She." Who says it is a guy? I didn't say it was a guy. I'm just using the word "He" because that is much more personal than "It." And anyway, it is a powerful force that is bigger than me. And I call that "dominant" and I call that "He." So, in that "He" is also the "She," the Mother, the All That Is. I have no problem with a dominant force. The only reason anybody has a problem with a dominant force is because they think they are going to be missing something. But that dominant force is who our Creator is, and our union and surrender into that dominant force will bring everything to you. So, I don't have any fear in being completely and thoroughly dominated. In fact, it's the only way to be. Domination. (The people laugh.) By God. We all just want to walk around like puppy dogs chasing after it – all of us.

So do you understand the open-mindedness needed on your spiritual quest to God, and how you have to be open to the very many ways He is coming to you? And you can't judge how somebody else is getting God. Who are you to say if they are meditating in a certain way and you are meditating in another way, that they are doing it right or you are doing it wrong? I mean, everybody has to let go of all their judgments about everybody else, and we have to all encourage each other to do their best. Take the guidance, take the help, and then go to God. Let God happen the way God happens for you, even to the point of your death; and at the point of your death, you will be ready for flight into whatever direction He is going at the time with you.

There is peace in finding your way Home, because you are ready for that flight, whatever that flight is. And it is an eternal flight, and you have no problem what it might look like, and what time or what color it might be or how it might look. It might look gray; it might look blue; it might be void; it might be personal; it might be impersonal. You are just ready, and you are feeling all of God. So you have to be very, very wide open, starting from right now, forevermore.

So I talk about freedom in this lifetime a lot, and I am going to talk about it even more, and I am going to talk about it even more and more and more, because that is what is available to everyone with the power and presence and energy that is coming in. You can make it. But I have to warn you, give up your concepts about what you think you are going to feel like when you are free. Even though I may tell you what it feels like, or I may tell you it is love and ecstasy beyond your comprehension, or it is whatever.

And sure, I am going to tell you all different ways of how it is feeling with me. If you then take what I say and start trying to have that happen to you, you will be doing nothing but conjuring up some kind of state of how you think it should feel. It is everything that I say, and you are going to know that. But you are only going to know by your own direct experience. You are only going to have your direct experience as you start to enter back into God. Whoever wants God and ultimate freedom won't settle for anything short of that. That is why they will succeed; they just want it all. They want to be showered by all the gifts and love of the Divine. And somewhere in people's hearts, they know that to be with God is to be showered by the Divine and all of the gifts and jewels that the Divine has to give.

But you see, even though people know that in their hearts, there are concepts that have been formed, like "Yeah. When you are with God it is going to be like this. Why would there ever be any pain? Why do you have to go through such a struggle?" I can tell you that what you are going through is going to bring you into the gems and jewels and gifts and showering of God's love. And it is because you are willing to open up on every level that God can shower every level of your being with Himself and His love.

You don't want to get hung up on your concepts about what freedom is. I am going to be talking about freedom a lot, because that is what I am here to do. I am here to talk to you about ultimate freedom, union with God, breaking the cycle of birth and death. If you cannot relate to that, you can relate to becoming one with God in this lifetime. You can relate to finding union with God and fulfilling that destiny while you are alive, and not arriving at your death without having fulfilled your destiny.

I am going to talk about freedom and breaking the cycle of birth and death. This transformation is not a "lightning flash" enlightenment situation that is going to happen. It is not going to be like, "Flash!" and then everything changes. It is not going to be like that. There are going to be many different types of "flashes" for everybody. With this current-day transformation that I am talking about, many different "light bulbs" are going to go on for many people all over the world.

The way you want to view your transformation is that every day you are doing everything you can do to become closer and closer to God. Every day you are doing all you can do to serve God more and to surrender to God more. And, in doing that, you know that every day you are becoming freer and are developing more awareness and more love.

Every day you want to do everything you can do, and if you don't, there is nobody to blame but yourself. Every day do all you can do to become closer to God, surrender to God, give to God, and then every day you will know that you are becoming freer and freer, achieving more and more awareness, and more and more love.

# Humility

*For humility, know this. You will never meet a person whom you are better than.*

GOURASANA

# Spiritual Ego and the Enlightenment Dream

*spoken on October 5, 1996*

It is very difficult to break free from this material world, from this illusion, from this dream. It is very difficult to break free and achieve ultimate freedom, to end the cycle of birth and death. It is very difficult. You have to want it more than anything. To let go, to give up, to surrender can be the easiest thing or the most difficult thing.

If you are searching for freedom, if you want to break free, if you want to find that eternal loving relationship and union with God once again, you have to have a consciousness that is so serious and sober in order to break free of the stranglehold of this illusion. "Serious and sober" doesn't mean that there is no laughter or that you are never lighthearted. It is just a depth of consciousness that you come into as a spiritual seeker when you are really ready to return Home. It is no easy journey, and it is not a matter to be taken lightly. So I use the words "serious and sober."

To break free requires current guidance from a live spiritual master. It is so difficult to break free even with the guidance of a live master who can help you see the illusion. If you want to break free in this lifetime, then you have to wake up and situate yourself properly on the Path where you can receive the guidance and the assistance that you need.

In order to receive the guidance from a master, you have to approach that master and listen from a state of humility. That means that you are receptive and open, and you understand that you do not know anything. That is why you are still seeking; you have not found your way Home yet. The proper consciousness always, even when you find your way, is to stand in humility. God is humility. A seeker has to sit in humility, and that is very hard for the ego to do. I am addressing this area of humility, because the subject that I want to talk to you about requires that you have some humility, or it will be very hard for you to hear me.

So try to situate yourself within, in humility. Do not be in a resistant place of, "I know. I've heard that before. I don't agree with what she is saying." All of this thinking has to be removed from your consciousness. You don't know. You haven't heard it before, not truly. The part of you that wants to say "I don't agree with her" is coming from your ego. I am speaking to you what is true in order to help you break free. And it is true for each and every one of you listening to this.

This is a very serious talk. I have a very simple point that I would like you to really grasp and then begin to work on diligently. It is very simple. Try to hear me.

Practically everything that you believe – that you have come to know as truth, that you have experienced, that you hold to be true and that you hang on to spiritually – practically everything that you are currently made up of is judgments, concepts, and beliefs. Practically everything that you think, and everything in all of your consciousness at this moment, is judgments, concepts, and beliefs. On the spiritual path Home, one of the most difficult things on the journey is to really understand that you are *full* of judgments, concepts, and beliefs. They all have to be let go of.

Some of you that are listening to this talk have been traveling on a spiritual path consciously for quite some time, and you believe that you have come to know something. A lot of you believe that you have come to realize many things. The fact is, you have created a very big spiritual ego and have locked yourself into a state of consciousness based on your experiences, all of which you need to let go of in order to find the truth.

You are going to be in for quite a shock when you start to let go and you start to see what I am talking about. So many of you have concepts about how transformation should look, how it should be, how you should be, how you are, what you think the path should be like, what God is like, what a spiritual master is like, what you will be like. You have so many concepts, judgments, and beliefs that are locked in place.

You have to be pried loose from these judgments, concepts, and beliefs because you believe that they are all true. It is one of the biggest traps for the spiritual seeker. It is one of the biggest traps for those of you who have been traveling a so-called spiritual path and sincerely endeavoring for God realization, for self realization, for union, for freedom. It is very hard for spiritual seekers to become humble and recognize, "My God, I have to let go of everything, even what I thought I knew. I have to let it all go, really let it go, because *I don't know.*" You are going to be shocked at what you have to let go of, and you are going to try to put up a fight of resistance from your spiritual ego that you have developed.

I am calling it a "spiritual ego." Everyone has ego, a being of illusion. But spiritual seekers have developed a very great spiritual ego. And it is mixed in with all of the states of consciousness and all of the ways of being that they have adopted along their spiritual journey; and based on all of the spiritual experiences they have had in the past, based on thinking they should be a certain way, and based on looking at someone that they hold to be enlightened. You have formed concept after concept after concept, and you have become that concept. It is quite a thick dream.

I like to call that dream the "enlightenment dream," the "enlightenment fantasy." The enlightenment fantasy has to die. It has you trapped. Those of you who have been searching for enlightenment, if you are sitting there thinking you are not trapped in an enlightenment dream on some level, then you can know that you are *definitely* trapped.

Those of you not on a spiritual path, or who have not traveled a spiritual path and are just embarking upon your journey, your biggest problem will be the judgments, concepts, and beliefs that you are going to try to develop along the way. You have to let go every step of the way. You cannot hang on to any state, to any way, to any end result of how you think it will be. You are going to form concepts out of what I am speaking to you right now. These judgments, concepts, and beliefs about what it is like to be with God, to be self-realized, to be enlightened are such a big trap. That word "enlightenment" has to practically be destroyed, because it has become such a dream.

These judgments, concepts, and beliefs that you have formed about spirituality are very thick. Everyone's concepts about self realization are not just from this lifetime; they are held collectively on this earth. They are worldwide concepts from every path and all the religions. It is all very mixed up. The reality is that you have to let go, give up, and surrender to God; and only then will you find your way Home. When you find your way, you will know the truth. And you cannot hang on to anything along the way. Right now you are forming a concept about what that means – to not hang on to anything along the way – so it is very difficult to speak about this area. At a later time, I am going to pull it apart with many different talks and point-by-point, talk about different ways that you are trapped.

Right now, I just want you to develop the humility to understand that you have to let go of all of the ingrained concepts, judgments, and beliefs that you have about self realization and union with God. You have to give up the enlightenment dream. Enlightenment is not what you think. It is not what some of you spiritual seekers have tried to turn yourselves into.

Start to let go of *all* of your judgments, concepts, and beliefs – all of them. Develop some humility, so you do not have resistance and defense.

The spiritual ego that you have developed is going to really fight to hang on. The spiritual ego thinks it knows, because of what you have experienced in the past. You have to let go of all the experiences. You have to let go of *everything*. One of the biggest ways the illusion is trapping the spiritual seekers is by trapping you into hanging on to what you *think* you have found, or developed, or become. It is a dream; it is just another dream. It is a spiritual dream. It is an enlightenment dream. And you have to let it go.

You are not going to like it when you are confronted with that illusion of the enlightenment dream. It is very deeply ingrained. Your concepts about God are deeply ingrained – how God will be or won't be, what it will be like to be with God. You have to let go. You have to let go, give up, and surender. You have to let go of practically everything that you are hanging on to that you think you know about spirituality, and what you think you are going to be like when you are Home.

If you are serious about breaking free, then develop the consciousness of a spiritual beginner. Always stay in that consciousness of a spiritual beginner. That way, you can always receive more truth and move forward. A beginner will sit there and listen, just listen, and let go. When illusions or concepts or misconceptions are pointed out, you will not have a fight for your way, for what you think, and what your truth is. There is no such thing as "your truth" and "my truth." There is only the truth. The truth is the truth.

Get ready to let go. Spend some time looking at all the spiritual areas about which you think you know something. Look at all the ways that you are as a spiritual being. Look at how you hold yourself to be spiritually. Examine it all and get ready, because you are going to come up against having to let go of all of it in order to make the opening so that you can break free.

This is one reason why you have to have a live spiritual master. How are you going to know that you are trapped and dreaming that you are in some kind of spiritual enlightened, or almost enlightened, state when you are just dreaming? Who will let you know about that? Who can see that?

There are a lot of people who are ready to wake up, but they have to be willing to let go of all the judgments, all the concepts, and all the beliefs of how it is going to be, how it is, how it already is, what they think. All of it has to go. As it is exposed to you and as you start to put up a fight, it will make more sense to you why

I keep saying, "Get ready. Become humble. Become a beginner." You have to let go of the very thing that you are hanging on to, thinking that it is truth. It is being challenged. You have to let it go, but you are hanging on. You don't want to let go, because you "know" it is the truth. You are feeling, "No, I'm not going to let this go, because I know this is the truth." Well, guess what? You have to let go, and what is the truth will remain. You have to let go of your grip on what you think you have found, and what you *think* is the truth. Nothing can happen to the truth.

In the end, you completely let go forever; you are never hanging on. You are going to even develop a concept about that, and then you are going to try to behave in a way that looks like that. It is practically doomed to even try to get the truth to you. That is why you have to be very serious and sober and listen from humility. You do not know. That is why you are searching. You must let go of everything in order to break free.

There is one quote that I like to use. It is in a book by a man named Joel Goldsmith. Basically, it is the truth. You are going to try to turn this into a concept also. You have no idea how deep these concepts and judgments run. You have no idea how very quickly you cling on to something and try to formulate a concept because you don't like the unknown. You do not like to fall into the mystery of your transformation. You would rather hang on to something. You have to be pried loose from everything.

The quote[1] by Joel Goldsmith is very simple:

> *As long as man has someone or something to which he can cling, he will not find God. No one is going to find God while he has anything on which to stand, anything to which he can hold, or anything about which he can think.*

[1] From Joel Goldsmith, *The Thunder of Silence*, [New York: Harper, 1961]

You are going to form concepts about this. One concept will be, "Wow, then I can't even hang on to having a spiritual master." That will be a new concept that you formed out of what I just spoke, and it is not true. Another concept you will create from the quote is related to the last part: "... or anything about which he can think." You develop a concept that you are not supposed to think.

You have concepts about meditation. You think that meditation has nothing to do with intelligence or thinking – when, the fact is, in meditation you tap into the greatest of all intelligence, the source from where all intelligence comes, and that is the Supreme Being, God. What kind of intelligence do you think encompasses all of God? Intelligence thinks.

So basically, you are in one big mess of concepts, judgments, and beliefs. All I want you to get from this talk is, please, situate yourself in humility and start to hear about all of the areas that you are trapped in. Pray to God to start to see all of the trappings, and start to let go. Have the consciousness of "I am going to do this. I'm going to break free, and I am going to let go of every single judgment, concept, and belief."

The judgments, concepts, and beliefs run very, very deep, and my biggest job is to cut through all of them. Because they are the biggest traps for spiritual seekers, and they are the biggest traps for those of you who have never even known you were a spiritual seeker. Your biggest trap, all along your spiritual path, will be that you will keep trying to hang on to what you just experienced. You have to keep letting go of all of it.

The enlightenment dream has to die. Your concepts, about what you think it is going to be like for you, have to be given up *constantly*. You do have to let go of everything; and you are going to form a concept about what *that* means. For instance, when I say you have to let go of "everything," then you start to think, "Oh, then I can't take care of myself. I can't take care of my family. I can't make any money. I can't keep a job. I can't have a house." I am not talking about that. You have to let go of all these things internally. We are talking about the bondage of your soul. The illusion is covering you over.

You have to let go, give up, and surrender, and you have to be very intelligent and responsible along the way. You have to get to the point where you are not fighting and resisting hearing and moving with the truth, or you are just simply not going to make it Home in this lifetime. You will make it Home in another lifetime.

If you want to make it Home in this lifetime, start to let go. Start to let go fast. Want to hear the truth. And when you hear it, rather than fight and defend yourself, just sit there, even though you can hardly stand it. Sit there, and know that now you are coming up against an area that has to be moved and let go of within your consciousness. Know that you are holding on so tightly and that it is the release of what you are holding on to that will bring you the truth. The release of the judgments, concepts, and beliefs will always bring you greater truth. The truth will never be lost as you let go. The truth will be found as you let go. But you are hanging on. Your grip on everything has to loosen. Work on letting go of the enlightenment dream nonsense.

This enlightenment dream is one of the biggest traps that is going on for spiritual seekers on all different paths and in the New Age movement. It is easier for a plumber who has never even meditated before, or thought about spirituality, or prayed, or given any endeavor to break free – it is easier for this person to break free than for a spiritual seeker that has been on a path for twenty years to break free, because the plumber has so little concept about it all, and because of all the spiritual concepts that the spiritual seeker has grabbed on to along the way. You are hanging on to all of the concepts, and you have to let them all go.

The enlightenment dream must die. It is a dream. You have formed a dream based on many experiences, based on what you have heard, based on what you have looked at, based on what you hope it will be like. That dream must go. Those of you who are hanging on to it, and who are in the middle of it, are not going to like for it to be exposed. The purpose of this talk is to prepare you to be humble and to approach the truth from humility. *Approach God in humility.*

Try to hear. Drop your defenses, because you are about to enter into an arena that is not going to be comfortable at all. Everything you hold to be true will be challenged, and you will have to let go of all of it in order to break free. Nothing will be missing, and everything is waiting for you, but you have to let go. You are going to be shocked when you start to see what you are trapped in. I am here to help you get out of the trap – for those who want to get out.

# Devotion

*spoken on March 31, 1996*

You *must* approach God in humility and in devotion if you want to again experience and live in the love of God.

I haven't spoken so much of the consciousness of devotion, because I automatically think that if someone is going after their beloved, if someone is wanting that connection to the Lord again, of course they would approach the love of their life with a devoted heart, despite all of the feelings that are going on within. Yes, there are feelings – the feeling of separation and so many other feelings – and you are being given plenty of avenues to release them. So don't let those feelings take away from your life of devotion to God. Your life in God has to become a life of devotion – your entire life, twenty-four hours a day. The only thing that satisfies you in this life is being in service and giving from a place of devotion.

This Path has come forth with an avenue for you to get your issues out, your problems out, your anger out, and your fears out. There are so many ways set up so you can release all of your feelings. The meditation itself, the Modern-Day Meditation, is set up so you can release all of your feelings. No one is asking you to deny your feelings, your anger, or your hatred. The whole path is set up so that you can release yourself from the darkness, the illusion that is covering your heart. But who you really are is devoted in service to God and to each other.

Do your meditation work and your spiritual practices, so that you can work through all of these areas of darkness in yourself. Work them through, open up, and release them. Live in a devoted state. Constantly live your life in devotion. Your relationships will change and your friendships will change when you start to live from an open heart, devoted to God.

I know you must be afraid that if you devote yourself to God, you will lose something. You think that devotion is some kind of submissive state, or some kind of state of consciousness in which you will be missing something if you live like that. But living in devotion is your natural way of being. It truly is, even though there is so much drama in your life, so many issues, and so many feelings in you.

Until you let go, you are going to be constantly moving through so much of this pettiness. While you are moving through the issues, the pettiness, the feelings, the anguish, the separation, the longing – every different thing that you are moving through – there needs to be one factor, a standard, that you live within as you are approaching the Lord. This is what you are doing by living in devotion. Once you click into that consciousness as you are approaching the Lord, you will change. Your heart will open. Because even though you don't know if He will be there, a part of you knows that He is there. You need to start to drop your ego enough so that you can live your life in devotion. Live so devoted that you are not waiting for something in return, not from God and not from anyone else that you are giving to.

Your giving has to be from a place of devotion and humility that you are giving for the other person's pleasure. You are giving for God's pleasure. You are not giving for your own satisfaction. Your true satisfaction comes when you are able to please the Lord. Your satisfaction comes when you feel that part of your heart just open and giving, and when you are giving to others you see their pleasure. There is just a satisfaction in you, because who you are is devoted. Who you are is a person that wants to give and share love, and that itself is what you receive. As you give love, you receive it within in the moment that you are giving. It is not that after you give, you see if the person liked what you did and acknowledged you and praised you, and so from that, then you have some good feeling. No, that is not giving; that is the ego. If you have an ego investment in your giving, you are not giving.

You should be humble, not unworthy; don't mix those two things up. "Humble" does not mean unworthy; "humble" is just a state of openness in which you approach God. You don't approach God hating God, even though you may have feelings of hate in you. You should just be working on releasing those feelings. The actions in your life and the way you live your life need to start to be that of living in a state of devotion and service, to each other and to His Mission.[1]

I have to pierce through a part of you now. In your heart, you know your devotion. Call it forth. Call it forth and live devoted to God, devoted to service, devoted to giving: always in devotion. You will be surprised how fast so many of the petty issues fall away when you do this. Again, you have plenty of time in meditation to seriously work through your issues and let go. Maybe

---

[1] Kalindi is referring to the universal spiritual teaching to give in service to the spiritual path from which you are deriving spiritual benefit and on which you are moving closer to God.

if you would start to live and wake up to the fact that you have just a short time in which to fall back into the arms of the Lord fully, you would allow your devotion to come forth. Maybe if you would wake up to what you are really doing, you would allow your devotion to come forth. You all know this principle of living in devotion. You all know it, because it is who you are.

The illusion would like you to be swallowed up in all of your anger and hatred and blame and resentments and hurtful feelings that the ego feels. The illusion wants to keep you in a soap-opera drama of all of those feelings endlessly, and never allow your true devotion to surface.

When you are really surrendered and you are really devoted, you are receiving God in that moment, even though you can't necessarily feel Him personally. It might take ten years to feel Him personally, but so what if it takes forty years? You remain single-focused. If you want God, if you want to be with the Lord again, you need to capture devotion and loving service. When you capture that and that becomes the way that you live your life, your whole life will change. When you are doing things to please the Lord, from devotion, your whole life will change. When you start to live from devotion and treat each other in your relationships from devotion and you are not sitting around with expectations constantly from each other, your whole life will change. You will then be with each other to give to each other, to share love with each other, to share truth with each other, to move toward God with each other.

If you will wake up to the fact that what your life is about is returning to the love of God, you will awaken the love of God in yourself that knows devotion. You will give it permission to come out, and you will start to live from that devoted love-of-God place within. You will live from that place, even though you have so much ego and so many feelings: jealousies, hatred, blame, fears – all of that. You are being given a way to feel those feelings and express that and release all of that, but your spiritual life should not be about wallowing in all of that darkness. Your day-to-day life should be about something bigger and greater and more loving than the darkness. You should live from the love that you are. Work through the darkness so that you can express the love more fully through yourself – from a real place, not from an ego place.

I just take it for granted that you will, of course, live in devotion as you approach God; of course you would be asking: "God, what do You need from me? What can I do for You? How can I help Your Mission? How can I be of more service?" If you have that consciousness with God throughout every waking hour of your daily life, you will see a difference in your relationships and friendships. There won't be so much fighting and strife and struggle. You won't have so many expectations from each other, and you will be able to work through issues. We are not saying for you to deny any of your other feelings, but there is an over-riding consciousness that you need to grasp in order to approach God and in order to live a life traveling toward God. You need to live from your love of God, even though you don't know if God is there or what that love feels like. I am talking to a part of your heart that knows devotion. When everything is said and done and you just open up, there is nothing but devotion in you.

You need to somehow find a way to live devoted as you are going through the death of the ego and going through all of your issues. Give to each other; love each other. Be surrendered to each other. Don't hold on in your egos with the attitude of, "Whose ego is going to win this war?" Try approaching each other in devotion and in humility, the same way you would approach God. Approach each other in a state of humility. If you can be in humility and devotion with each other, and in the honesty that is called for on this path, you will see how fast there will be loving relationships, support, and exchanges with each other, in friendships and in man-woman relationships.

The key is that you have to be living in devotion to God. You know what devotion is, and you fear devotion because you fear surrender. You think if you are devoted, then you will be giving up your power somehow. But I tell you, it is in devotion, in living without expectation, in humility, in love, and in service that you find everything. Have no expectation from God and no expectation from each other.

If everyone in the Mission is devoted, everyone will, of course, be giving such focus to what their service is for God and doing that service to perfection. Each area of God's Mission and of your life will be handled in a conscious, aware place when you live from devotion. If you were devoted to God, you would be serving everything and paying attention in every way to every aspect of your life as you would if He were standing in front of you – just imagine.

It has to start, though, with you devoted to the Lord, in service and in love. You have plenty of time to get down on the floor and scream and cry in your meditations, when you feel all of your darkness that keeps you separate from living in the devoted heart that you really are. Please try to hear this.

I am just shocked to see the selfishness that is going on in the quest for the love of God. In your transformation, don't go after God and God realization and self realization from a selfish place. You will never, ever find the love of God by approaching God from selfishness. You need to approach God from your true state. You need to find that true state of humble devotion while you have all of your ego and all of your darkness. That devotion has to override everything; you need to live from devotion. Then your meditation work will go much deeper, much faster, and you will not fall prey to so many of the petty issues. You will just work through them very quickly, because you will come to relish living with your heart devoted to God and to each other.

Don't take this teaching of devotion and then turn it into some mushy, airy-fairy, nonsensical, unreal way of being. I am not asking you to muster up an unreal state. I am just speaking straight to your heart and to your soul. Start to wake up and open your eyes. Sit in meditation and feel, "My God, everything I do, I do it all for You." Feel your devotion. Live in your devotion. And when you are doing your meditation and working through your ego, your illusions, and your fears, take the time to work through it all.

But live your life devoted, because before you know it, time will run out. You live devoted to God every single day without expectation, just in devotion, in service, in surrender, with a prayer in your heart for freedom and for God. Live with a prayer in your heart for mankind, and be doing everything you can do every day to break freer and freer of the illusion, of the ego, of the traps that you are caught in. Live in a devoted-to-God state, and out of that, your transformation will move very quickly into the love of God.

I am just astonished at the ego and how the ego is so absorbed in wanting recognition. That ego is ruling you, even though you are on a path to God. The ego wants recognition so badly that you are afraid to be devoted to God. You want God to recognize you.

You want someone to recognize that you are serving God. You want something other than just to be loving and devoted to God and, in that state, to go through your transformation.

Don't wait for ten years to be devoted. Find that place of devotion in your heart now, even though you have a hardness around your heart. Find a deeper place anyway, and approach your spiritual quest, your spiritual path, your spiritual life, your journey to God from a devoted place. Wake up! You are an inch away from His embrace. How could you be living in any other way than in devotion?

You are somehow forgetting that you are traveling back into God. You are waiting for something to be given to you, something to be proven to you, before you will be devoted, and you are making a very, very big mistake. Don't wait. Don't wait for the future. Find a way to live in service and devotion to God, starting now.

Every day you must live with a devoted heart, despite the hardships of the "death of your ego" transformation that you are going through. It is because of your devotion to God that you will be carried through. You will be just taken by the hand and carried through the hardest times, because despite how ugly it gets inside of you, you remain devoted.

Just start that right now and never leave that. Start it from a real place, not a phony place "just because Kalindi said to be devoted." I am asking you to really find that place, because you all know it very well. It is within that place of devotion, and living in your human expression with spirit entering you and living in you and expressing itself through you, that you find satisfaction; and that is because you are living in total devotion to the Lord.

Devotion to the Lord, *now*, not when you get the Lord. When you are trying to go after a lover, or a boyfriend or a girlfriend, you don't go after that person hating that person. You approach that person from your love, from the truest part of yourself, and you begin to give to that person.

So you have to get this. This is very critical: Live your life in devotion to God twenty-four hours a day, and you will see a big difference in how you relate with people, in how you relate with God's Mission, and in how you relate to your transformation. You will see a very big difference in how fast God reciprocates with you. It doesn't come out of your expectation, because there is none. That is how He reciprocates with you so quickly, because you just live to serve. You live to give from your devoted heart to God.

Try to hear this. You know what I am talking about. It is not a wimped-out place; it is not an unworthy lifestyle. It is in your true nature. So try to take a stand against the illusion, especially with this Path. You are being guided into the depths of so much darkness within that you have to be situated within your devotion and your love for God, or you will never make it; you will be swallowed up inside of your transformation because you just went into all of those ugly dark places, but you forgot all about why you were doing it. You are doing it because you are returning into the Lord, into His arms, into His love. Don't lose sight of that, and try to wake that up in yourself. You know what I am talking about. The love is your strength, and the love is the only power that there is. It is not some airy-fairy type of love, it is very real love. So do your best and try to hear.

# How to Receive Guidance from a Master

*spoken on February 10, 1996*

I have talked to you many times about the need for guidance in order to break free from the illusion. I would like to speak to you now about how to receive the guidance from a spiritual master through the written word of a master, through the spoken word of a master, and through the master's guidance coming through the programs of the path that the master is bringing forth. There needs to be some understanding about how to receive guidance.

You come to trust a spiritual master more and more through your connection to God. The only way you can truly surrender to the guidance of a master is because of your surrender to God. You feel God so deeply, and as time goes by, you come to trust more and more the master that you have connected to or that God has brought to you, because you know that master is bringing you the truth that you have asked for. In direct response to your prayer to God, your master comes.

Spiritual seekers are, by nature, most often very serious and attentive, and are listening for truth and wanting to hear. When they sit with a master or listen to a master or follow the programs of a master, there is a natural underlying feeling of receptivity and of wanting to hear the truth. So there is a feeling in the disciple or in the student or in the seeker of wanting to hear.

And when you do hear, you immediately want to act and do everything that the master says. You listen, and when you listen, you listen from a place of hearing the words and hearing the guidance and hearing the direction. You hear from your mind, and you hear from your heart, and you hear from your consciousness.

Oftentimes, though, because you are wanting the truth so badly and wanting to know the direction to go in, you listen and, in a mindless way, just start to do what the master said. You just do it like a parrot, or just do it and copy it, believing that if you just do it and copy it exactly like the master said, then you will break free, or then you will make it.

Now in some areas of guidance, it is necessary to take the guidance to heart and do exactly what the master has said. But, more than literally trying to understand each word and then implementing that guidance, you need to understand that the guidance is a direction to guide you within. The guidance brings you hints at the direction that you should go within so that you can discover the truth within yourself. There is some guidance that is very practical – spiritual practices, for example, which you need to somehow find a way to incorporate into your life. That is just very practical guidance of something that you need to do.

Another example is my guidance on meditation and coming to meditation: meditate twice a week, come on time, do not leave before the meditation is over, do not ever miss a meditation unless there is a really good excuse, and that the illusion will even try to have you be sick in order to keep you from coming to the

meditations. Of course, the sincere seeker will take that guidance
– never be late, never leave early, always come, there is very rarely
an excuse – and they will be stalwart because I said it, and they
are going to listen to that guidance.

I want to use that as an example, because this is an area where
I am giving you a big hint at a consciousness to achieve and a
spiritual practice to put into place that is so important for you.
And the communication you need to receive is the importance
of meditation, the importance of coming to meditation, the importance of being on time, the importance of not leaving. And I
am also giving you guidance about how the illusion will try to
stop you from meditation.

But you need to be very mindful in your application of that
guidance, because there very well may be a reason why you
can't come to every meditation, a good valid reason. Or you truly
may be sick. So you need to pay attention and take the guidance
as a strong hint at the direction that you need to go in. But don't
take it so literally that, for instance, you come to meditation
anyway even though you are truly sick because you heard me
say the illusion will try to have you be sick, and it is just the
illusion. Or during meditation you may be sick and need to
leave, and you will remember that I said, "Well, the illusion wants
you to get a headache or get sick and have you leave." There
may be some times that you are feeling very physically sick in
meditation, and you *should* go home and care for your body.
Do you see?

So take the feeling behind my guidance, take the hint, take the
direction, and begin to apply it with seriousness and sincerity, but
don't be fanatical and become mindless and don't take care of
yourself. You need to take care of yourself on the path.

Another example is my speaking about the illusion and bringing guidance to you about the illusion. Your state of consciousness with hearing me needs to be that you are a seeker and you are coming to a spiritual master. You need to be in a state of humility and receptivity and openness to hear. And you need to hear from a consciousness in which you recognize that you don't know. Even those of you who think you know a lot spiritually, you need to sit in a place of open receptivity so that you can hear what is being spoken and digest it and take it in.

For some of you, what I say will resonate and validate what you already know and give you more understanding and clarity on what you already know. For some of you, I will be speaking truths that are very foreign to your consciousness at this point, because there are simply layers of illusion that haven't fallen away for you to be able to hear some of the things that I say. For example, when I make a statement, "This is a place of suffering. No matter how good it gets, it is a place of suffering." That is an example of a truth that you need to sit and take in. Even though you don't understand exactly what I mean by that, you need to just take it in and not walk around and start repeating or believing what I said. You then need to start your inner process of looking within, of trying to come to realize, and to really understand this point that I made.

There is a disciple who, after four years into her transformation, was able to tell me, "Kalindi, I understand now what you mean. I can see that it is suffering; it is all suffering, no matter how good it gets." She realized this after four years of her own process of self-discovery. She listened to me and listened for four years in receptivity. Even though every time I would speak certain things, and they didn't quite register, a part of her could kind of feel the truth, but couldn't understand fully yet. But she was receptive because she knew I was speaking truth, even though she couldn't understand it or even agree with it. She knew I have come from God to deliver truth. So even though she disagreed or couldn't understand, she was in the proper state of receptivity throughout the years to hear. Then she had to go within and do her necessary work to find the truth within herself.

I am here to bring many teachings of truth, some of which you will understand, and some of which will take you years of inner search and quest and moving through illusion to understand from a realized place what I am talking about. That is why it is important that you listen to the talks many times, because it might not be for four years that you really grasp what I am talking about. Then when you hear it from a realized place inside yourself, you begin to shift and open up to true consciousness and true awareness from a realized state.

The talks and the words spoken by a master or a spiritual teacher are important to listen to many times as you evolve. They are a hint at the direction to go in to find the truth for yourself. You need to go within, into your inner struggle, to find the truth and let the words of the master be there to guide you and direct you. It is not that you believe everything that you hear and negate what you feel. It is that you are receptive and you know, "Okay, there is truth here. I don't understand it, but I am not saying *my* truth is true, I just need to do my work now to find the truth within myself." So the master says many things to trigger you, to help you go deep within through years of inner struggle and battle, so that you come to realize the truth directly for yourself.

There are times that I say something very powerfully because I am speaking to cut through the illusion. And I may say, "You need to do such and such." I bring this same flavor through to all of you as a group as I do to an individual. And you, as part of the group, receive it in the same way the individual does – your ego is threatened; you feel like your life is threatened; you hear me; you want to act on what I say; you don't know exactly what to do, but you are going do it, and you are in a frenzy trying to do it.

More of what you need to do when you listen to me is try to hear what I am saying, and then go within and see how it applies to your life. Go within and see how what I am saying can help you in your life, if it can, and how to incorporate it into your life. If it is a spiritual truth, just take it in and just keep moving spiritually, and eventually you will come to understand through realization.

I often speak very pointedly, very sharply, without much explanation. Then it is yours to go within and try to find out what was I talking about. That causes you to go into deep reflection so that you can come to find the truth. I guide you or point you in a certain direction. When I am speaking to you, first of all, you can't let your fear be the filter that my guidance comes through, because then you can't hear me properly. You have to be mature and strong enough to hear me, even though it may be annihilating to you. If you let your fear be present, you can't hear my underlying intent and direction.

I will give you another example that happened with someone I gave guidance to. I was interacting with a disciple, and I could feel her slight distance and some fear in her. I told the disciple, "Come closer; come further; move faster now; don't let the fear stop you," because I could feel her distance. Then I told her, "You need to get through this by Monday." That gave her three or four days. "Get through it by Monday. Scream your way through it, and just go through it." My guidance came to her very powerfully. She was very open to it, and she set out to accomplish what I had spoken. What needed to be heard, though, was the *feeling* and the *intent* and the *direction* of what I said.

The next day she called me to get clarity on that guidance. She said, "Kalindi, I want clarification on the guidance that you left me with, because you told me to scream my way through, and I've been sick for four days. Because of my lungs, I don't think I can scream." What I could feel in her was that she was just stuck in fear, and I had to tell her, "You needed to get the underlying *intent* behind what I was saying. I was giving you direction. What you need to do is scream your way through it so that you can drop to a deeper depth and just go fast. That is how you get to the deeper place that you are looking for now. Screaming is the way you break through that part. When I said, 'Do it by Monday,' the *feeling* was just, 'Come on; you can do it fast.'"

But she left with such a literal translation and was ready to go and act upon my guidance, and the fact of the matter is, her body was sick and she needed to rest. So she needed to just take in what I said, get the intent. "Okay, the way I get through this next part is that I have to scream." That was direct guidance about how you are going to get to a deeper place. You just scream your way through it in deep meditation. But she took it so literally that, "Okay, by Monday I have to do this, and I have to go home and scream now." But what I really meant was, the *direction* was, "Don't let your fear stop you. You are stuck in fear. Scream your way through it, and do it fast and just come. You have to come now." So, she could take the underlying intent of, "I have no time to waste; I have to move through this; I have to go fast. My key is to scream my way to the next depth." But she can take one week or a week and a half, or however long it takes, and rest her body and then know the direction that she needs to go in.

So I bring guidance through sometimes very powerfully: "You need to do this and you need to do it now." I bring that through many times. So what you need to do when I bring guidance like that is try to capture the feeling that I am bringing and then see how to bring that about in your life, how to have that happen in your life, and know that the illusion doesn't want you to listen to me. That is why you need to act upon what I say, and listen to the guidance. But you also need to get the underlying feeling of my words and the underlying hint of the direction I am guiding you in and then go within and find your way. Find within, what is it? How was that guidance that Kalindi gave me trying to direct me?

My guidance is a hint and a direction. There are keys in there. There are keys in everything I speak, and there is truth about the illusion in everything I speak. Your place in hearing me needs to be very receptive and very open, even though your ego is challenged, and your current understandings are challenged. Rather than stick to your guns, "Well, I'm right, and I don't believe her," you need to have the consciousness of, "I don't quite agree or understand, but I am open, and I am going to go on my search, and I will keep listening to those words and talks and keep going and keep going and keep going and keep going."

Eventually, as you break through illusions, you will understand what I am talking about. But the truth I speak is not for you to believe and accept because I said it. It is for you to take in and then just do your spiritual work, and you will come to realize truth for yourself, and you will understand what I speak as time goes by.

So there are two things: there is the truth I speak, which you may or may not understand, and which oftentimes is going to trigger you. I am a divine trigger to bother the illusion in you, to bother your current beliefs and understandings and judgments and concepts, to cut away all of that on a deep level so that you are oftentimes disturbed. Then it is your job to go within in meditation, and work through everything, and find the truth for yourself within. This process takes years.

The other point is that when I am giving a direct instruction of what you need to do and *you need to do it*, you need to take that also. When I say it like that, you need to really take that in and understand, "Okay, I need to do this." Then you need to see how you can apply it to your life. I never mean for you to neglect the care and well-being of your physical body, ever. If you are really sick, stay in bed and take care of yourself. If you are really sick in meditation, by all means, leave early. But just try to understand what I was saying is that the illusion will have you many times just feeling tired, having a headache, give you many excuses to leave, because there is such a resistance to giving your time to God for three hours twice a week.[1]

I am trying to give you the understanding about the illusion that will try to stop you from meditating, and at the same time you need to be mindful and pay attention to your own well-being. Don't blindly take my guidance. Try to hear from a soul place within yourself. For instance, don't plan social events and evenings of pleasure for yourself when it is supposed to be a meditation night. Start to revolve your life as much as possible around your meditations. Try to understand the underlying message and the intent. Then see how you can apply that in your life. Be diligent with it, and do it with seriousness, but with mindful thought and consideration.

[1] The group meditation schedule at the time of the talk.

Also know that while you are using your mindful thought and consideration, the illusion may be entering into your mindful thought and consideration, and trying to get you to make decisions that you may think are the truth, but the illusion is in there a little bit so you don't quite grasp the seriousness of the guidance I am bringing forth. I bring it forth powerfully to try to get it into you, because the illusion does not want you to hear it. Then if you are serious, it is your job to hear it, to understand it, and then to move with it in a way that is mindful, and out of an understanding that you are following my guidance. And you may or may not agree with the truth that I speak about the illusion. And that is just going to take time.

I say things to trigger you. I say things to force you to go within in deep search so that you can find the truth for yourself. My guidance is not being brought to you so that you will become blind followers. I am bringing guidance to give you a hint, a powerful hint, at the direction that you need to go in order to succeed. Then you need to take that guidance mindfully and see how to place it in your life along with the truth that I speak about God and about the illusion.

You just need to be receptive. If you are a seeker and you are listening to someone who knows – and you don't even know if I know, but a part of your heart can feel me – you just need to receive it and receive it and receive it and then do your inner work on yourself to come to direct knowledge and realization in yourself.

Listening to my talks and reading my books and Gourasana's books, and listening to The Lady's and Jim's talks,[2] over and over

---

[2] The Lady and Jim St. James: see Glossary, the Core.

will help you as the years go by to come into your own direct realization; but you have to realize truth for it to be truth. You won't have truth by believing truth that is spoken to you. So I am speaking to you, and I am here to destroy the illusion and hammer away at the illusion and the ego. I am here to bring forth what is sometimes disturbing information to guide you to go within and find the truth. I am also here to bring direct guidance about what you need to do. And you have to do it. You have to do it. But then you have to sit down mindfully and discover how you are going to do it.

In your meditation work and in your inner quest, it is going to take years of the illusion being broken down, being broken apart, so you can realize the truth. But my job is to create so much desire, burning desire, in you to go within in quest of truth and God – and nothing short of that. When I bring direct guidance, grab hold of my underlying intent, and don't be literal with it to the point that you miss what the true message was, and just doing something very literal and not capturing what I was really telling you.

There are windows of opportunity for spiritual movement that are going to be happening all along the years now. That is one way God in His power is working now. There will be windows of opportunity that God opens for you and He says, "Come on, jump." And I may know that that window is coming, and I may say to the whole Mission, "Come on, in two weeks. Come on, get jumping very quickly. Two weeks, come on." And some of you will hear that and some of you won't. So when I say something like, "Come on, there is a window of opportunity coming, a window of time that you can slip through into a great shift of consciousness," you want to take it very seriously and just move very fast, because this is a time I mean it very literally. I may say it to the whole Mission, and then whoever can hear and whoever is ready will have the opportunity to jump through that window of opportunity.

So I hope you can understand a little bit from this talk about the guidance, how to receive Kalindi's guidance. Try to hear the underlying intent and message, and act upon that and fit that into your life. And know that while I give you space to do that, the illusion will try to take advantage of that and have you not really grasp my guidance in a way that you embrace it and have it change your life. The illusion is working so hard to have you not hear me, so I say it powerfully. I mean for you to follow it, but you need to take it within in a mindful way and then find out how to apply it in your life. Find out how to take the hint of the direction and have it work so that you come closer to God and so that you go deeper in your meditation work. It will take you time to understand some of the spiritual truths that I speak.

# Inner Strength

*Don't be weak and discouraged*
*and give up. You can all be strong.*
*Pray for the strength.*

GOURASANA

*Cling to God's hand*
*when you are working through your darkness;*
*cling onto God like never before.*
*Do not ever go into the dark world of illusion*
*and try to leave God behind.*
*Stay with God, now that you have God*
*so much. Never leave Him, ever.*
*That is your part as a seeker of the Lord.*
*Once you have found Him,*
*you have to keep looking His way,*
*stronger and stronger and stronger;*
*hold onto Him stronger and stronger*
*instead of holding on*
*to the illusion so strongly.*

KALINDI

# Transformation
# and Care of the Body

*spoken on October 8, 1996*

The illusion is a force that is constantly working against you. It is working against your success, both materially and spiritually. At times, you fall for its alluring nature. The illusion is a tricky force. That is its job – to be tricky.

You have also heard me say that everyone is coming Home. That is just a fact. Everyone will eventually end the cycle of birth and death and return Home. It is just a matter of when the soul is ready.

Life is no easy journey. The human condition is made up of one big struggle. It is a struggle for existence, struggle for survival, struggle for enough money, struggle for health. So much endeavor is needed just to support the human condition. Then there are the "three dreads" – disease, old age, and death. They are un-avoidable. If you take birth, you have to face these three dreads. That is just a fact. Everyone will grow old, everyone will become diseased in some way, and everyone will die.

Some people are less fortunate than others in the area of health and disease and with what happens in their bodies in this lifetime and in each lifetime. Some people have poor health; some people have good health. Some people, as they grow old, are confronted with terrible disease and a lot of discomfort on their journey to death and then rebirth. Some people grow old and they do not have a disease; they just endure old age and the suffering of old age, the body wearing down. These things are just facts, whether you are transforming or not transforming, breaking free or not breaking free.

Some people choose to live their lives with all of their effort totally focused on making sure that their survival is intact. They are constantly focused on making enough money, thinking that making money is going to be the way out of the suffering of this place. They think, "If I have enough money, I'll be safe." Some people put so much focus on the body and the health of the body, to an extreme, in hopes of never having a disease come their way. Some people that have put the greatest focus on health and physical well-being still become diseased with horrible diseases.

You are not going to get rid of human suffering as long as you are in a human body. The only way to get rid of the suffering is to wake up, awaken fully to what is really going on in the material condition and find your way to freedom, so you do not have to repeat life in the material world again and again.

There is a specific point that I want to get across to you in this talk. If you are choosing to go through the transformation of waking up out of the illusion and returning to God fully in this lifetime, as you are transforming and start to open your eyes and your heart and start to face everything within yourself and everything that is going on in the world, one of the more difficult things is to have all areas of your life work harmoniously so that you can transform, so that you can awaken, so that this can be your last lifetime. This point relates to my talk "No Time to Waste";[1] maybe you can understand that there is no time to waste from a different point of view now. *There is no time to waste;* and it is difficult to have everything working in your life harmoniously so that you can transform at a rapid enough rate to break free. It is difficult; so what are you going to do about it? Everything has to become workable so that you can move – within yourself – through your illusions, so that you can serve God in the way that He is asking you.

In your transformation, you will be moving through what you have to move through to get out of the illusion, and you will be serving God in the way God is asking you. To do that requires that you pay attention, use the Modern-Day Meditation, and use your intelligence to set everything up in your life so that you can do those two things – work on yourself and do your service for the Lord. That is a pretty full package right there: to work on your illusions to break free, and to serve the Lord.

In order to do this, *you have to pay attention to your body and its needs.* People in general know the importance of exercise and taking care of the body. The illusion, practically speaking, has most people negligent in this area. The illusion keeps them too lazy to take the proper thought and the proper time to see what is best for the body. But when you are on a path of rigorous transformation, you have to take care of your body. You cannot use your transformation and your service to God as an excuse that you do not have time to take care of your body and your well-being. You do have the time. You have the time to accomplish everything that God wants you to accomplish.

---

[1] Kalindi's talk "No Time to Waste," is in *The Simple Path to God* Series.

Taking care of your body means you need to exercise. It means seeing health practitioners when you need to. Eat properly. *You do not have time to waste.* You have your livelihood to take care of. There really is no room for any resistance, because the resistance inside of you is actually taking up so much of your energy and so much of your time. If you know that you are going for spiritual freedom, then put your energies toward going for it. That means all aspects of your life must be seen to, nothing neglected.

If you are going for spiritual freedom, give up the resistance to your transformation. Give up the resistance to surrendering; give up the fight. This fight is taking so much of your energy, and you could be using that energy to do something positive to help you in your transformation. You could be doing something positive to help you with your livelihood, to help you with the health of your body, to help you with your service to God. You do not really have time for resistance on the path of surrender.

There is kicking and screaming that you go through – as you are letting go of the illusion – that you cannot help. But your consciousness needs to be "I'm just doing it." Your consciousness needs to be of sweet and willing surrender: "I'm just going for it; no matter what it feels like to let go of the illusion, I am going for it, and I have to take care of all aspects of my life."

Taking care of your body means making some time to relax. The reason you cannot relax or have some quiet time for yourself is because of your resistance. Pay attention to your body. Do not neglect the call of your body and what your body needs. Do not blame your transformation, your service to God, and your material job as the excuses why you didn't exercise, why you didn't go to the doctor, why you didn't eat properly.

If you use all of your energy to positively move forward, you will be able to take care of every single area of your life. It is imperative that you take care of every area of your life in general; but if you are traveling a rigorous spiritual path, it becomes even more important.

You are not going to escape the "three dreads," no matter what. Whether you are transforming into freedom or whether you are going through another lifetime of moving toward Home, more freedom, more consciousness, you are not going to escape the three dreads. You are not going to escape inevitable death or the phone call: "This is the disease that is getting you." You are not going to escape inevitable sicknesses, headaches, ingrown toenails, stomachaches, indigestion. So many things go on with the body.

Some people have more things happen with their bodies, some people have less. That is why you each have to do the Modern-Day Meditation; look into every area of your life, find out what works for you, and then put it into action. "Okay, my job starts at nine in the morning. I get off work and I don't get home until six o'clock. When will I exercise? When do I go to meditations? How do I eat properly?" You have to look into all of these things, and then you cannot let the illusion stop you from being in action. The illusion doesn't want you to exercise. The illusion doesn't want you to take care of yourself.

As you give yourself more and more to God, and as you awaken more and more, you are going to feel such a pull on you to give more and more and more. That is the way it is. God fills you with more energy and more desire to give more and more. This means you have to focus even more on how to take care of your body so that you can rise to the occasion. Do not let the illusion put fear inside of you and tell you "Oh, if you get so busy, and you do so much for your transformation and do so much for God, then you might get sick. You might get too stressed out, and you might not be able to take it." NO. You can take it with the energy of the Lord; with God on your side, you can take whatever it is that God is asking of you.

He is also asking of you to take care of the vessel called your body that is actually living here. I tell you that this is a place of suffering; that you are never going to find the happiness you are looking for here; that it is going to all come from within, with your connection to God. I tell you that this material world is nothing but one big, bad situation. The illusion will have you become very negative when you hear this type of truth. You become negative and give up hope, and you give up taking care of the body also. But the opposite has to happen: You have to take fine care of the body, and that care has to become finer and finer.

You have the time to do everything you need to do. If you give up all of your resistance, you will see how much time you have. You have time to give every way He wants you to give. You have time to work and take care of your livelihood. You have time to transform. You have time to meditate.

Your whole life has to become a walking Modern-Day Meditation. You have to be using all of your time and all of your efforts toward transformation, toward the world's transformation, toward all of the people that you are helping, toward what you are doing for God. Your time and effort also has to be going toward taking care of your body, so that you have as much fitness and well-being as possible.

That doesn't mean you are going to have your whole focus be on taking care of your body in hopes that your body can just live forever. You have to match and meet and rise to the occasion of the demands on your body. Not only do you have to do a general amount of exercise; there are other little things that you have to do also. You have to be tuned in to what you need to do for your body.

You also have to get out of this syndrome of blame and resentment when one of the "dreads" comes, or the disease and sickness comes. You want to blame, "Well, if I weren't working so hard and if I weren't giving my life to God or my transformation, I wouldn't be sick." *That is not true.* You don't get cancer because you gave your life to transformation. Cancer comes your way because that is what is coming your way. You cannot stop these things from happening.

You can stop some things from happening by proper care of the body. Some people need more sleep than other people, and you need to be sure that you get the sleep that you need and the rest that you need. As you become more and more filled with the energy of God, the amount of rest your body needs will change. Maybe you will need more sleep; maybe you will need less sleep. You will always be able to rise to the occasion of what God is asking for.

You need to pay close attention to every aspect of your life. Are you situated in the right job for your livelihood? Is it conducive to your transformation and to your giving to God in the way God wants you to give? And are you taking proper care of your body? Take care of your body like it is a car. Oil it. Grease it. Put gasoline in it. Wash it. Clean it. Keep it lubricated. Feed it. Exercise it. Take care of your body. That is my main point. *Take care of your body.* Do not use taking care of your body as an excuse to not do your transformation: "I'm doing so much for God and so much in my transformation; I have to stop that, because I have to take care of my body." You simply need to incorporate everything.

This is a place of suffering. As you awaken more and more and look at this place of suffering, you are going to be disgusted and feel hopeless so many times. But as you are awakening, and as you are looking and seeing what is really going on here and giving up hope of finding happiness in this material world, don't neglect the fact that you are here. This place is where you are going to awaken so you can get out. This place is where you are going to help God bring love into this world, to bring healing into this world. Your body is the vehicle in which you have to go through your transformation. So take care of it.

You are not going to find happiness here, but that doesn't mean you shouldn't surround your room and your environment with things of beauty so that you can sit in a place that has some beauty in it. It doesn't take a lot of money, either, to put a flower in your room and have cleanliness about you.

As you are waking up and facing the hopelessness of the material condition, do not take that to the degree that you give up so much and you lose your motivation to take care of yourself, give to yourself, and nurture yourself. Your body is a vessel of God. It is the only one you have right now. If you are going to break free in this lifetime, you had better take care of it! Taking care of it properly does not mean that you are not going to get sick, and that you are not going to become diseased; because you may.

You are going to leave your body at some point. Either you are going to be ready to leave your body with conscious departure or not – depending on how far you get spiritually, and whether you let go, give up, and surrender in this lifetime.

There is so much illusion inhibiting people from taking proper care of their bodies. And when you start to face the predicament that you are in, there is so much fear.

You are probably never going to have exactly the body that you want, exactly the way that you want it. Even though you may exercise and may have good health, something is going to come that actually makes the whole thing not quite as palatable as you would like it to be. As you get older, you are going to face the fact that the body is growing older. That is a fact. You cannot blame the fact that your body grows older and you die on your transformation and on your service to God.

You want to have a very sweet and willing surrender in your transformation so that you do not waste one second of a day. You need to do a lot of things every day. You have your livelihood to take care of. You have your service to God that you have to do. You have your transformation that you have to do. You have your body to take care of. You have other people that you have to take care of. Your life is quite full if you are living a life for God. You have to take care of everything.

Give up the resistance to the path, and just know that it is going to be startling and a little painful to walk in this world while you are waking up and seeing the horror that is going on within you and outside of you. The only way out is to get out. But that is how it is going to be, walking the path into truth. You are walking back into the Kingdom of God. That means that you are leaving this material world, but you have to be here and transform and do a lot of work on yourself and do a lot for God as you are transforming. You need to live as long as possible so that you can make it all the way Home while you are alive. You do not know when you are going to die. So who has any time to waste?

The general health and well-being of the body should be a focus. Pay attention to what your body needs. Everyone should be living like this in life, even if you aren't transforming on a spiritual path. The general motivation in everyday life is just to have a nice body, which isn't enough motivation. So much revolves around having a nice body, but this isn't enough motivation for most people to take proper care of the body. The illusion completely sucks almost everyone under so they do not take proper care of the body.

But the motivation to take care of your body is different when you are living a life for God. On the path to awakening, one thing you must do is to take care of the physical body. "I am awakening in this body in this lifetime. I'm going to take care of it while I am used as a vessel for God, used even more than I thought I could be used." (God is going to use you more than you ever thought you could be used.) As you are transforming, pay attention to what your body needs.

Do you get the point? What time do you have to waste? There is no time to sit around trying to take a break, watching TV or wallowing around in all of your endless unworthiness. Get a stationary bike and listen to a lecture talk of truth; or get on a treadmill or a stair stepper or go for a run. You can figure it all out if you give your life to God, live for God, do it all for God. Do it all for God. Take care of your body.

If you find out that you have cancer or that you have a disease now, don't blame anybody or anything. Just start to wake up to the fact that these things are going to happen to you. And *before* they start happening, and while you have health and you are not dying yet, take all of your time to transform and break free. And within that, take care of all aspects of your life. Do not just take care of your material life and then neglect your spiritual life. You have to do everything at once. That is what the Modern-Day Meditation is all about. It is to help you figure out all the many material and spiritual details of your life to take care of. You have to do it all.

There are some situations where you may have a job that actually is not good for your physical health. Maybe you are lifting boxes and you have a bad back. Maybe you have a bad neck, and in your job you are working with computers, which is making your neck worse. You have to meditate and find out what is a better job, because your body cannot take the one you have.

As you open up more and more and let the energy of God come into you, you are going to be surprised at what you are actually able to do. Once the resistance is gone and God can flow in you, then you will be able to do what you are being confronted with in your life; you will be able to get enough sleep, get enough rest, get enough relaxation. You will be able to help all the people, help God's Mission, do your transformation. Let go of all of your illusions. Get your heart ripped open. All of it is going to happen, and that is why you have no time to waste.

Look what you have to accomplish. You have to be very sharp and very aware and very alert. You are going to become fully aware as you awaken. That means you will become aware of everything that is going on, and you will see to the very fine details of your life and other people's lives. Not only will you see to your life, you will have enough energy to help other people, so that they can see how to best take care of their lives within their transformations. So the transformation is not easy, but you can't be stopped. You have to keep going.

Do not be fooled by the illusion. "Well, I have to slow down; because if I don't slow down, then I am going to break down."

No. If you feel like you are going to break down, you need to meditate to find out how to properly put everything in place so that you can go forward. Do the things that you are accurately supposed to be doing in your life. Give up your resistance, and you will find out that you have so much more space, so much more room to do everything that you need to do.

When I find out that I have a disease or that death is coming, I'm not going to blame it on the fact that I was working 24 hours a day for God. And while I am working 24 hours a day for God, I am taking care of every single aspect of my life. I have to do that. I have to exercise. I have to eat what I need to eat when I need to eat. I have to know when I need to sleep. I have to know when I need to take a day to rest and regroup so that I can go forward. I live my life like that. When disease comes and death comes, I will not blame it on anyone or any circumstance or any situation. I know these things will happen. Every day I see to it that I take care of everything that needs to be taken care of for the body.

You also need to do that, but not at the expense of putting your transformation on hold, or putting your service to God on hold, or putting your livelihood on hold. You have to do it all. The Modern-Day Meditation will help you to do it all.

When I speak to you that this is a place of suffering and to give up all hope on having yourself be fulfilled by anything in this world, that does not mean that you can't look at a flower and see the beauty in the flower It just means that you see both; you see the duality. You see the beauty and the suffering.

Try to understand what I am trying to convey. When I speak of the hopelessness of this material world and that the only way out of the suffering is to get out of the illusion, to break free, do not be fooled by the illusion. Do not become discouraged and lost and lose all motivation. You have to have *great* motivation. You are embarking upon the greatest of all journeys. You have to become spiritual giants, like you are practicing for the Olympics. You have to become very intensely focused every second of the day. When it is time to relax, you become very focused on "Nothing is getting in my space today, because today is my day of relaxation." You have to take care of your body and everything in your life every day. It all has to become integrated.

God is going to ask a lot of you. It is a big thing that you are doing to break free. You do not just do it for yourself. You do it for the world. That means God asks a lot of you. That means that you have to use all of your energy to do everything to take care of yourself while you are being used to serve God and to awaken yourself. Try to understand.

# No Escaping Reality

*spoken on March 5, 1996*

I want to address a misconception. And try to hear me. Wake up. Open up your ears. Open up your mind. Open up your consciousness. Open up your heart. Try to hear this one. Try to hear this one, because this is a big, major misconception.

I have to talk to you about ultimate freedom and about breaking free from the illusion. And about no rebirth, about getting out, about going Home, because that's what I'm here to do.

I'm like a travel agent. I'm here to help you to go on the greatest vacation that's going to happen very soon for you. It's called departure from material existence into eternal existence where there is no more death. So I'm like a travel agent that's preparing you for that departure – if you want a conscious departure. So I have to speak to you about breaking free and ultimate freedom and going Home because that's what I'm here to do. I'm here to guide those of you Home who want to go Home and break free.

But breaking free, returning Home, preparing for conscious departure, does not mean that you check out of material life while you're living this human experience. Breaking free from the illusion and preparing for conscious departure – you will have to *fully enter* the material world and *live* this experience. You'll have to stand in this world in total responsibility, fully alive, fully open, here, now. You have to get fully here to get fully out.

And getting fully here as you move through your transformation doesn't mean that when you get fully here, then you engage in all types of illusion. You get fully here and you live as a being of truth, a beacon of love and light, here in your human experience. It's the highest human achievement possible, to break free.

So there is no such thing as trying to check out or "I want to just get out of here. I can't stand it here." Yes, that is a feeling that's in there in order to break free. But the actual act of breaking free doesn't give you an avenue to check out, to cop out, to become just a lazy bum, to not care about responsibility. It's the total opposite. You become *very* conscious. You become *very* capable. You become fully aware. You are able to help *so many people*, not just yourself. And for the most part right now, all anybody can do is just take care of their own self, if they can even do that. So there's this desire in some people when they hear about breaking free, that it's going to be this escape route from all your problems.

But you're going to have to *face* all of your problems. You're going to have to face your inabilities to function. You're going to have to face all of that, and your full true self will emerge within your humanness and will be *fully* here and *fully* present and *fully* aware and *fully* functioning and *fully* able. And you won't be sitting around wishing for death because there will be no more death.

Death won't be a way out either. There is no way out. There is no cop out. There is no checking out. There is no oblivion. There is becoming present, becoming conscious, becoming aware, becoming fully who you are in God for eternity. There is aliveness. You become alive and you live forever. You understand that death is nothing more than releasing you fully into more capacity. That's only if you're fully aware, if you're fully realized; otherwise death is death. There's more death. But in a fully aware state, death is no longer there. There's just a departure from material existence into more of who you are. But if you're not fully realized, if you're not fully aware, then death will bring you more of the same: suffering, material consciousness.

So I'm trying to address this area of the spiritual seekers that use this path to ultimate freedom as a cop out to not be responsible. And I'll tell you, in the end with God, you are *so responsible*. You are so responsible that you give your life to the care of the whole world. If you could, you would take care of every single person in this world. You *care so much*. You are so conscious. You are so aware. You are so much love. You are so much vitality. You are not sitting around wishing that you would be dead or wishing you could get out. Once you break free, you *know* you are out. You know you are out of the illusion. It is no longer binding you, but you live in so much responsibility and consciousness.

Your last lifetime, in order to break free, means you bring all of God's presence into this world in so much glory to stand as that beacon of truth. I'm not leading a group of people that are trying to check out – go off and live in some huts or caves or mountains or whatever you think I'm talking about with ultimate freedom. I just want to use striking words: it's just like *blasphemous* to think that to break free of the illusion, to be fully with God means that you check out of all responsibility and you don't care about people, nor do you care about yourself. And you just want to get out because you can't stand it anymore. And so you speak about getting out in a way where you're trying to cop out from responsibility. You're trying to cop out from life.

The reality is that you're going to live life in a fully conscious, fully aware state: full love, full light, full truth – right here, right now. God is *now*. God is not in the future. God is now. If at the time of your departure, the death of your body, you want *life* and you really want out of the material suffering, then you had better wake up *here, now*. And *get here now* with God, *now*. Or you won't be there at death. You will continue to be in a suffering state at death.

So to get out of material existence, to be prepared for conscious departure, into eternal life, where you care even *more* – to be with God, to be in eternity, to be in eternal life, to break free from the cycle of birth and death – you only come to a place where you are *more* able to give, *more* able to help, because you are not confined by a material body.

You can't understand this from your mind – what it's like to be with God, what it's like to be free. But this is one understanding that you've got to get. And it has to stop with whoever of you are thinking that this path to ultimate freedom, breaking free, means that you're just going to cop out, check out, be irresponsible, be in la la bliss land.

To break free means you break in. You break the illusion and you become your highest human potential. And you stand in it for the service of love and truth and light. You stand in it to help the world. And you don't sit around wishing that you would die tomorrow. You take *great care* of your human vessel. You have great focus to live this human life for as long as possible because you can see how much help is needed here. You don't think about wanting to die to get out. You're already out once you're in – in a free state.

Once you break free from the illusion and enter into your human-ness, in a free state – free of the illusion, here to serve God – you are Home. You are with Him. No more ego. No more separate will: just the will of God. You're here and you're ready for de-parture. You know Home. You know what's going on. But you're no longer in this place of misery and suffering, thinking that somehow getting out is going to be the answer to your many problems. Your breaking free of human existence, of returning to human form is going to be the answer to a big problem, because human existence is nothing but suffering. It's a very difficult situ-ation. But you don't get out of here by blanking out or copping out. You have to come into a fully aware, fully conscious, fully alive state while you are alive.

And your transformations to get there are going to be somewhat difficult. And the difficulty of your transformation is what's going to bring more consciousness into you, more awareness into you, more responsibility into you, because the transformation out of the illusion is *so* difficult and trying at times that you have got to become strong in order to get through it. Strong and vulnerable, or God can't come. And it's God that's entering. It's your true self that's emerging. So your transformations are part of what will have you come into a place where you are just strong in this world, strong for mankind, strong inside of yourself. And you're no longer worried about getting out because you *are* out. You find freedom, and you look forward to the day of your departure. Not because you're trying to cop out of your responsibility. You know that when you depart this material existence, how much more you'll be able to even give.

There are so many things that you know when you're fully awak-ened, when you're in a fully aware state. There's no sense in me telling you about all that because you'll just turn it into concepts.

As I speak of ultimate freedom and as a travel agent – which is what you can think of me as – I'm trying to prepare you for *conscious departure*. And while I'm preparing you and helping you go through your transformations, it's your job to help other people to prepare. There are only a few years in between now and that great event. And if you're going to make it and if you're going to be ready, you have to break free from the illusion. In order to break free from the illusion – or breaking free from the illusion means that you will be here fully, free, standing in your human expression. Free from the bondage of the illusion. One with God. *One with God.*

There is no such thing as copping out or checking out or voiding out or being irresponsible. If you have problems with being responsible, you are never going to make it to freedom, because you have to be so responsible in order to make it to freedom. You have to have your wits about you. You have to have your brains about you. You have to have your consciousness about you. You have to be able to function. You have to be able to be real. You have to be able to be fully here. You have to be able to be fully present. There is such a demand on you as a human being in order to walk the fire of true spiritual transformation back to God.

*Please, try to understand.* I'm trying to prepare you so that you don't take birth *again*, so that you can get free from this place of suffering. But while you're here, part of your last lifetime, part of breaking free is to fully enter and fully have the human experience for what it is meant to be: that you stand in God's glory to bring His truth and His love to mankind. Your last lifetime is *very important*, and you won't leave without *fully* being present.

Getting free means you become fully here. It's happening right *now*. It's not happening later. You've broken free and it's happening right now. The love and ecstasy of God is happening *right now.* Your freedom is *right now.* If you could possibly live for two hundred years, you're fine. You take such good care of yourself so you can last as long as possible, so you could be of service. And you also know the glory of your departure and that you've made it.

But please, don't be one of these kinds of spiritual seekers that are just trying to check out, because they can't stand the responsibility of being a human being. It's the opposite. It's the total opposite. And I know the feeling of being trapped in the illusion and you just want to get out. You just wish that death was here. You just wish that you could get out, get out, get out. But don't misinterpret what I mean by getting out; getting out, breaking free – yes. Let's plan your conscious departure. You're going on a vacation – your death is imminent, you're leaving your body. Are you going to die or are you going into eternal life?

Based on your consciousness at the time of the departure out of this body, you either stay where you are in your consciousness and move into another suit, another body, another vehicle that just transports that same consciousness that you died with. Or you're ready, you're free, and you know you're free, and you're living here free. And you know you're walking in a world of illusion. Just because you're free doesn't mean the illusion isn't happening everywhere around you. You're walking in a world of illusion, but you're walking in the truth inside with God. You're a vehicle of His love and light walking in this world of darkness, and you have much to accomplish.

So if you don't want to be responsible – if you think freedom, ultimate freedom, if you think planning for your departure, if you think spiritual transformation somehow means that you can check out or be irresponsible or use spiritual transformation as an excuse to your already illusory situation, that you're just wanting to check out because you can hardly stand the illusion anymore. ... So you would love to use spirituality as an excuse to check out; but you are not going to use *this path* to check out. Because this path is here to *break you free*. And to break you free means that has to happen *now*. And that means you have to *get here*, and you have to get here for the *will of the Lord*. And you *live for God*. And you live for mankind. And you live with purpose. And you live with love. And you live with truth. And you live with compassion. And you live with passion. And you live to want to serve.

You have *great purpose* in your last lifetime. It's a *glorious* thing to be in your last lifetime because of the difference that you'll make for the world because of the responsibility that you come to live in. The responsibility is *very great*. And all power is given unto you and comes into you from God in your union with God.

So I know this feeling that makes this consciousness come about that you want to check out or that your spiritual life is going to somehow get you out of this illusion. You have a concept of what getting out means while you're alive. Getting out while you're alive means you break in, into full awareness and full consciousness and full connection.

If you don't want to be responsible, and you don't want to do the necessary transformational work on yourself, and you don't feel like you *can* take care of yourself and stand to serve and give, you better work on those points before you enter into deep spiritual transformation that's going to break you free.

And I'm being a little bit heavy with this point. Because those of you who are trying to escape, you give God a bad name. You give freedom a bad name. You give ultimate freedom a bad name. Who in the world that is conscious and wants God's pure love to come into this world is going to respond to a group of people that are just trying to check out? Do you think that I'm checked out? Do you know that 24 hours a day I'm living in so much responsibility? I care so much. The Lady cares so much. Jim cares so much. Hana cares so much. All of those of you who are making it are caring so much and are so responsible. That is what mankind is waiting to see: Is this *really* a path to freedom?

Because they're tired of seeing these spiritual paths of spiritual seekers just checking out on life.

Try checking in on life. Try checking in – and check in, in full awareness. Go through your transformations so that you can stand up and live in this life *fully* aware, *fully* conscious, *fully* in union, in great humility, and in tremendous responsibility.

There's no escaping reality. There's no escaping God consciousness – other than ignorance. And it comes from ignorance that you want to check out and that you think a spiritual path is going to give you an avenue to check out. It's not. *This* is a path to ultimate freedom, and that means ultimate consciousness, full awareness. And will you be prepared for conscious departure? Yes – if you break free. And to break free means you *break in.* And you live and walk in this world as a bearer of light and truth. You get in, in order to get out. You find life eternal while you are alive. You know Home while you are alive. And then you live in the glory of what is inside of you to bring it to mankind. And you touch the world in many ways with your love and with your light and with your truth that is yours in God.

And then we run into another misconception, and that is people think it's their egos that are going to become illuminated or enlightened. And the ego really, truly has to die. And that happens in the fire of true spiritual transformation. And for someone who really wants truth, they will not go for the trap of the ego-enlightenment nonsense. The ego dies and the true self lives. The ego does not become enlightened. The ego is all illusion.

So you have to undergo the annihilation of the ego, which is a difficult transformation. But it brings you fully here – fully present, fully now, fully here, free from the bondage of the illusion – and stands you in this world to serve, to give, to love. And you don't have any time to think about getting out anymore. You are out. You know you're out. You know you're Home. You know Home. *You are Home.* And then there's so much work to do. And you live in so much responsibility. You can't even imagine the state that you live in when you're with God.

So stop thinking that to break free means you're going to cop out. And so then you start copping out on your path. Cop in. Get in. Get in here. Get responsible. Get going. Stop being babies! When are you going to give? When are you going to live for God? When are you going to take care for your life? When are you going to be responsible?

*It's time to wake up.* If you want to escape through spirituality, go somewhere else. This is not an escape. This is about consciousness coming in and you awakening into full consciousness, full truth, union with God – coming through your transformation into that state. And all the while in your transformation, there's more and more consciousness coming in constantly.

I hope you can just get the point. If you want the responsibility of living your life for God and getting in as you get out, breaking out to break in, to be prepared for conscious departure, you're going to have your eyes open. You're going to have light coming out of your eyes – not some dreamy, blissed-out, trance-like state coming out of your eyes. You're going to be a clear channel, clear vessel. People will look into your eyes and see strength and light and clarity. Light – not some dreamy, enlightenment nonsense-state that you've conjured up, how you think you should look or be. It's real. It's real and you're here.

And in order to get to that point, you go through a very intense transformation of the death of the ego. And through that, you find all of your strength. But you should head into it knowing that you're not escaping. You're coming into your fullness by walking through your transformation – even though at times during your trans-formation, you don't know *how* you're going to make it. But that makes you call on God more; that makes you want your self more.

To be prepared for conscious departure, you have to get all the way here right now. You have to be here *now*, so if your death would happen *now*, you're already prepared. Your bags are packed. Everything's tidy. Everything's ready. You're finished. You've done what you came here to do. And you are just there – you are already there. The body just falls off. *You are already Home.* That's what it means to be prepared for conscious departure.

But what it looks like when your bags are packed and everything is ready to go, you just are so tidy of a package that you have full space, full potential, to give your whole life to service to mankind until God says, "Okay. Now it's time. Come on." But until then, you are *completely* in service – completely in service to God to help mankind.

So go through your transformations. And I know they get difficult sometimes. But you go through your transformation, taking care of your life, taking care of other people – give to other people, give in the service of God, live to give, live to care. Even when your transformation is at its wits' bottom end, be responsible. Take care of your material life. Take care of other people. Give to God. Do it all and do it now. And keep doing it all and do it all now. And that will be what saves you during your transformation, so that you don't get sucked under by the illusion. Live in responsibility because in the end, to be fully conscious, you are fully responsible, fully capable, fully able. You know that checking out – you can't. What? What? How foolish.

Give up your concepts of enlightenment. Give them up. They're not accurate. You're dreaming, all because you want to escape into some oblivious fantasy of bliss or something. And I'll tell you, bliss is there. It's all there, but it's not what you think. It's not what you think at all, and it is everything. It is love. It is ecstasy. It is peace. It is glory. It is bliss. It is Samadhi. It is every different thing, *but it's not anything like what you think.*

So you just need to know: You want to be prepared for conscious departure? You want to get out in this lifetime? *Get here.* Get here now while your transformation is going on. Get here on two feet in responsibility to take care of yourself and to give in the service of God. Live to serve. Live to give in total responsibility. Take care of yourself. And take care of everyone around you. And then reach out even further *while* your transformation is going on. And stop this nonsense of just copping out or checking out or using your spiritual transformation as an excuse to not be able to function.

If you're going to try to use spiritual transformation as an excuse not to function, don't stay on this path. This is a path of high functioning. And your transformation is what will give you more and more and more of God as you go through your transformation. So you come through into *such* an ability to function.

And you function from pure light and love in your state of freedom. And you live in this world for God, for mankind.

So you want to break free? Get in. Get here. Get now. Get responsible. Do it now. *Do it now.* Muster up all of your willpower and *do it now.* When it's hard for you in your transformation, you are in battle with the illusion. The illusion wants you to think that you can't, you can't, you can't, you can't, you can't. And you take action, and you *do* go through your transformation and be in service. Take care of your own life and give.

Don't use your spiritual transformation – or breaking free, breaking out, preparing for conscious departure, ultimate freedom – don't use that for an excuse to further your illusion of laziness and irresponsibility. That's what we're trying to break. So when I talk about breaking free and breaking out, I'm trying to prepare you for that day so that you have found your way out of this place of suffering. But you live your last lifetime to bring it all the way in. You bring it *in* for mankind. You bring God's love and light and truth in, *purely* for mankind.

And I say "purely" because if you let that word stick in your mind, then you will know, "My God, it can't be this ego. This ego has to go because if it's going to be pure, there can't be any ego." So you pray to purely bring it in. And "My God, let me live a long time. Help me to break free and let me live a long time so that I can help in this world. And I want to be prepared. I want to wake up. I want it to happen now so that I am prepared. If my death should come in one month, I'm already ready."

So try to see if you can understand the points that I've tried to cover in this talk. I'm very intense about this area. Get in. Get here. Get real. Get with it. Get responsible. Stop the excuses.

# Ability to Be in Action

*Effort is the key to advancement.*

GOURASANA

*All you need to concern yourself with
is that you are doing
everything you can do, every single day,
to become closer to God,
more surrendered to God,
and more giving in the service of God –
and watch yourself every day
achieve more awareness, more consciousness,
and become freer and freer.*

KALINDI

# Living in God Consciousness

*spoken on February 18, 1996*

What does it even mean, "to live a God-conscious life"? In order to live a God-conscious life, one thing that is unavoidable is change. While you are seeking God, you need to live your life on your spiritual path from a God-conscious place. You live the same way when you are living fully with God. So one thing that is unavoidable, whether you are a seeker or in union with God, is change; and that will always be the case. Change is unavoidable.

To grow, to evolve, to be with God, to move with God, to move through the illusion in order to be with God, requires change. Change is something that scares everyone. It challenges your security; it challenges the ground you stand on. It is pretty rare that you find people having "two hands up" to change. Living in a state of "Now do this. Now you have to do that. Now do this. ..." is very rare. It is very rare to live in a state of change. I realize that for some of you it is going to take years of your own transformation to come to understand, through your own realization, the beauty and the glory of change. Through your own experience, you are going to see what happens to you. Everything is going to change in everyone's life on so many levels. There is a lot of resistance to that change, but as time goes by and there is more trust and faith, change will be embraced and not feared so much.

You are moving out of the illusion, and this means everything is going to change. Because you are currently living in illusion, and in many cases, in total service and surrender to the illusion, you are going to have to go through a lot of changes in order to live a God-conscious life. It doesn't need to take years to live the way that you need to in a God-conscious life, to change the things that you need to change in order to live in a God-conscious way that is in service to God, not in service to the illusion. It doesn't need to take years to come to live in a God-conscious lifestyle.

Some of you may take years to be willing to make the changes necessary, but a lot of you won't have fear and will make the changes that you need to make. As soon as you can see that your desire and your love for God is so great, you will say, "Yes, I'm going to change that right away." As soon as you see that something needs to be changed in order to have your life be lived in a more God-conscious way, then you immediately change. And you want to try to come to that place as early on in the path as you can. I realize it may take some of you two or three years, but it doesn't have to; you can just let go. You can search within and start to feel from a place of devotion in your heart how you can live your entire life at a very high standard, in a God-conscious way of living. I don't mean in a materially rich way; I mean in a consciousness-rich way.

There are many behaviors that you need to let go of that are habits, that are ways of being, ways of doing things. You just need to change. There are things in your environment that are not conducive to promoting God consciousness around you in your life; so you need to change your environment. There are relationships that you are involved in, friendships that you are involved in, people that you are involved with that are not necessarily conducive to the current movement that you are going through, and that actually disturb your consciousness very much. There is a way, from a God-conscious place, to arrange everything: your friendships, your lifestyle, your environment. There is a way to break all of your old habits and just change. Most often it means radical change is needed in order to move into new consciousness.

You are going to go through a lot of changes. You want to be living a life of consciousness, high consciousness – not just when you come to meditate, not just when you are with people that are being conscious at that moment or during that evening. You want to practice your high level of consciousness across the board in your life. For those of you who have staffed the Seminar,[1] it is a good example of God consciousness in the level of care and devotion and love that you need to hold within yourself. When you are staffing the Seminar, you are meticulous about all of the surroundings at the Seminar; you have so much care about your appearance, taking care to look nice for God and the people who come. This is a good example of higher consciousness that you come into for that period of time. The tricky thing is: how can you bring that consciousness into every area of your life across the board during your transformation? How can you raise your consciousness to a higher state?

People are hanging on to so many old ways of being and so many old habits. You just have to make a conscious choice, "I'm just going to change. I'm going to change all these things. I'm going to change all these different ways of being that are keeping me

---

[1] Kalindi offers transformational seminars; people who have participated in one are welcome to volunteer as staff and continue receiving the teachings in this way.

bound to an old feeling in the illusion." For example, you can change the type of clothing that you wear to match the new feelings that you have as you transform.

You have to make a decision to change so many habits, to look at the illusion and see it is affecting you in every area of your life. Look at the way you walk and the way you talk. Look at the way you engage in your ego. You allow yourself to walk and talk in illusion, and you know it is your ego that you are engaging in. You can feel it. You allow yourself to engage in that kind of separation. The illusion is creeping into every area of your life, and you allow it to happen.

When you take the stand to make changes to live at a higher level of God consciousness, you will be making a direct statement to the illusion of "I am no longer going to engage in the ego. I am not going to engage in separation. I am not going to dress in a way that the illusion has me feeling unworthy. I am not going to have my environment feeling less than the highest standard of devotion and beauty that I can create around myself."

You have to change your old way of being. And you cannot just do it as an exercise because I am telling you that you need to change your habits, your environment, and your clothes, and that you need to stop engaging in the ego and stop allowing the illusion to create separation. I can tell you that you can just let go, but letting go means you really do let go. You can't just do this as an exercise. You have to get it from somewhere deep inside of you that you are ready to change your life. You have to get it that you are ready to live differently. You have to not be afraid to make some changes in order for a higher level of consciousness to emerge in your lifestyle, to have a more God-conscious place of living, and to have more consciousness in all areas of your life.

Bring God into all areas of your life. What would that look like? What would you need to do? What do you need to change? Do the Modern-Day Meditation; meditate on this area. Ask, "How can I live a more God-conscious life? What do I need to change in the different areas of my life in order to bring my life up to a higher standard of living for God every second of the day?" You have to make a conscious choice that you want to do that. Once you make that conscious choice and you go within in your meditation and you look around in your life, you will be able to see so many things that you can do to change.

In order to do this, you have to actually wake up a part of your consciousness that is sleepy, the part of your consciousness that hasn't already made this change. You cannot do it as an exercise; you have to do it as a choice. You have to decide, "I am now going to change because I want to live my life in a God-conscious higher state, not in service of the illusion."

You come to a higher state of consciousness that is more conducive to remembering God twenty-four hours a day, rather than living in the state of old habits that just pull you down into a lower kind of material consciousness, living for the illusion. It will require a lot of change, and I don't want to get detailed into the areas of the changes. I think that you all need to go within, and from a conscious place, make the decision, "I'm going to change everything so that I live for God, through and through, in all areas of my life." You will all individually be able to find what you need to do. You will start to look around, and once you change one area, you will start to see the sloppiness of another area, and see that they don't line up together. You will see the higher consciousness that you have in one area, and that will make you have to bring another area up – which will mean change.

All of this happens because you want it to happen. You have to want it, you have to say "yes," you have to have desire. You have to want to live your life in a way as conducive as possible for your God-realization. You are living a life of incredible transformation.

When will you start to change all areas of your life? When will you break all the old habits so that they are congruent with your consciousness? As you are stepping up, as you are going deeper within, just keep coming to a higher level of consciousness in all areas of your life. It is a matter of making a conscious choice. It is not that someone is going to tell you that you have to do something. You will know that you are living for God once you make the conscious choice to live in devotion and to live in higher consciousness – in a consciousness that is focused on the Divine, that reminds you every moment of the day that you are living for God, in service to God. This is a different consciousness that lifts you out of the illusion. Just to make the choice and make the changes and to live in God consciousness completely removes so much illusion.

It can't be an artificial thing: "Oh, I will just change my room around. Oh, I will just put that picture up. Oh, I will just do that..." You might have to do some things like that to get yourself moving, and you will end up changing many things in that way, but it is different when you change it from a heartfelt choice than when you change it because somebody told you that you should change it. If you want to change and come to a higher consciousness, you will. I want to get across to you that you need to come to a higher state of living, a different kind of consciousness, in which you are living your entire life, through and through, from just a higher level of consciousness.

Don't be sloppy. Live your whole life for God. When you cook, when you are cooking for someone, the consciousness should be with so much love, that you are offering that food to God. That should be the feeling in you. If you were offering food to God, what care and love would you be putting into the cooking? If you were preparing your room or your living room or your house for God, what would be the consciousness that you would be living in? If you were interacting with a friend, and you knew that you were engaging with a part of God, even though there is illusion there with that person, what loving state would you have in your consciousness when you communicated with your friend?

Your consciousness will change when you want it to change. When you are ready for higher consciousness, when you are ready to stop engaging in the illusion, when you are ready to stop allowing the ego to have its way, when you are ready to stop the separation, you will start to change things in your life that you need to change in order to live from a more conscious place, a more God-conscious way of living.

Some of you have been moving spiritually for a very long time, and it is critical now that you take this teaching to heart. Some of you are brand new to this work. Some of you have come to this work and already know this consciousness that I speak of, and you already live it. But some people don't. There is a difference in material consciousness and spiritual consciousness. There is a big difference.

See if you can take this teaching into your meditation – and take it to heart. If you are not already living and changing and moving in the way that I have spoken about, search within and see when you can make that choice. When can you make those changes that you need to make? When? What do you need to do? What will help you? And little by little, there are going to be so many changes that happen in your life. If you knew all of the changes right off the bat, you would never buy the package called "God."

So God gives you as much as you can take. And you always have free will and choice until you finally surrender. And then in your surrender, still, it is free will, because you are the one that surrendered.

You have choice in the matter. You have choice to go for higher consciousness and change. Change is something that you will grow accustomed to and want, because you will start to see that change means growth. Growth means more light. Light means more love. It all means more God.

See if you can take this seriously. What changes do you need to make? What habits do you need to break? And will you? Will you really do it from the proper consciousness, so that when you make changes, it changes your consciousness? It is not just an exercise. You change internally along with the external change, along with breaking the habits. You change because you want to, because you want to live in God consciousness; you want a higher standard in your consciousness throughout your entire life.

Do not let the fear stop you. And start to reconcile within yourself on some level that you will be going through constant change and transformation. That is the way of God. See if you can embrace the way of God of change, movement, growth, forward evolution. You want this consciousness I am talking to you about. You really want it, and the illusion does not want you to make this jump, because everything will change in your life once you decide to stop allowing the illusion to have control. The illusion is in many very practical areas of your life.

Those of you who are serious, go within; do the needful. Change because you want to change. Embrace change. Embrace it because you understand what change really means. The Modern-Day Meditation will totally help you in every single area of your life, and it will constantly help you to come to higher and higher consciousness if you will just go within, ask, listen, and then do the needful.

# Freer and Freer Each Day

*spoken on March 2, 1996*

I understand that, depending on the state of illusion you are in, when I speak words like "spiritual freedom," "ultimate freedom," "return Home," "break free from the illusion," you don't necessarily understand what I am talking about. Different people are situated in various degrees of awareness and light, so according to that, they can hear more or less of what I say. For some of you, there is no context for you to put those words in. There is no way that you can understand them anyway, because they are beyond comprehension. The truth cannot be put into words; it cannot. So everything that is coming out of my mouth to guide you is to give you a hint at the direction that you should go, so you can directly come to realize the truth for yourself.

It is only through direct realization that you will come to understand freedom and the true realm of existence. It is not a state, and it is not a concept. It is nothing that you can conjure up with your mind. It is nothing that you can shoot for. So don't let my words of "breaking free," "returning Home in this lifetime" stop you just because you don't understand what those words mean. You cannot understand what they mean. You can't sit in the illusion and understand the true realm. The only way you can understand is by letting go of the illusion and entering into the true realm of existence. In order to do that, you have to have a tremendous amount of trust and faith. And your faith and trust will increase as your awareness increases. So you can know one thing: when I speak those words, I speak from the ultimate place of *"Come Home. Come. I am calling from where your Home is waiting for you. There is such a thing as freedom."*

When I call to you like that, try to hear from your heart. Then on your part, all that you can do is every day move through more and more illusion and come into more consciousness and awareness, every day freer and freer. Every day, come into more consciousness, more love, more honesty, more truth, more dedication, more commitment to your path, and more devotion to God, moving through layers and layers of illusion. Your day-to-day path just needs to be every day, freer and freer; "Every day, I'm doing as much as I can."

The illusion doesn't fall away overnight. It takes time, steady work, and serious desire. It takes seekers with fiber, with intense desire, with dedication, and with commitment to walk through the fire of spiritual transformation to actually achieve self realization. It doesn't come easily. It is completely possible. There is so much assistance from God. There is so much guidance. There is so much power available directly from the Source. But it doesn't come easily; the path to self realization is not easy by any means.

You are arriving into a state of full truth. You will come to understand what I speak about when I speak about "Home" and "union" and the "true realm." You will totally be immersed in that place. Those of you that are undergoing transformation, don't be frustrated and try to figure out what I'm talking about and try to get to some end result. Just every day, pay attention and do what you need to do to move through more illusion and to become freer and closer to God every day of your life. If you are doing everything that you can do every day, then you are doing what you need to do.

It is a very difficult undertaking. You need to take care of yourself. You need to take very good care of yourself, and you need to take care of each other. Only you will know, but there are times when you need to be easy on yourself and know when to relax the effort. You are all going to be constantly pushing so hard to break free of the next illusion, the next obstacle on your quest, so you need to know when it is time for you to take a little break for a few days and just relax the effort a little bit. You need to know when to rest and how to take care of your body.

Those of you who are serious and want freedom (even though you don't know what freedom is) need to create a certain lifestyle conducive to achieving it. You need to create a lifestyle that is as peaceful as possible and as free from anxiety as possible. You need to create a lifestyle that is revolving around the fact that your main endeavor is breaking free from this illusion and that everything in your life is designed to support that endeavor. If you want to come to a state of full awareness, if you want to break free, that is how you need to set up your life. You need to set it up with the least number of distractions possible while being totally responsible for all areas of your life.

Breaking free means that you become filled by the presence of God. It means that your ego dies and the true part of you lives. The true part of you lives to house the full presence of God. Through your humanness, that presence of God can be brought into this world and be given. You can stand in pure truth, love, and light and let it come forth. To break free means the presence of God will fill you ever-increasingly, but the ego has to get out of the way in order for it to be pure. The ego dies to allow the full presence of God to enter. Your true self stands in union with the presence of God, and then the truth and love are here.

When the presence of God fills you, you know what freedom is. There is no more question about what breaking free is, what Home is, what the true realm is. In the presence of God, there is no more question in your mind about this illusory plane of existence being anything but illusion and suffering, despite the fact that there is some happiness to be had here. There is no more question. You live in the love and light of God fully. You can't get there overnight. It takes time. You have to decide that you are going for transformation. You have to decide that you are going for it, and then you have to aim your arrow high and then go through the transformation that you are going to have to go through.

You can't see and you don't understand the most important assistance that is going on to help you to break free. It is coming directly from God and working with you in ways that are beyond your comprehension. He is helping you. True understanding comes from your heart. It doesn't come from the words. The real communication comes from a very deep place, even deeper than the heart. The real communication comes from a place of hearing and knowing, and that is where you need to be situated when listening to me or to any true teacher who is speaking truth to you.

You have to do the work. All of the words that are coming to you and all of the guidance that is coming to you are to guide you to surrender to God. There is a movement from within that wants to happen to you, that is beyond meditation. It is beyond everything, and it is connected to God's energy that is here to take you out of the illusion into the truth. You have to do the work.

I hear so many times from people, "What do you mean by 'freedom'? What is 'ultimate freedom'? What is 'breaking free'? What is 'Home'? I don't believe all those things!" You don't believe all those things because you can't believe them. They have to be directly experienced, and that happens over time through serious spiritual transformation that is not easy.

I want to end this talk with just a few things for you to remember. One is about another quality that you need to embrace, that has to always be at the surface of your being. This is because transformation of this nature is difficult. You are going to be letting go of the entire illusion. Practically speaking, everything in your life will change in order for you to come into the truth. There is a very important quality that you have to learn to live with every day that will make all the difference to your – I want to say happiness, but it's not material happiness. It will make all the difference to your path. Though your path will be difficult, there will be pleasure in your path. And the quality that you need to have to live in that pleasure is gratitude.

You need to let the quality of gratitude really come through you. As you are going through your transformation and things are difficult, side by side you need to recognize the light that you are receiving. You need to recognize the spiritual movement that is happening to you. You need to recognize all of the people that God has put in your life to help you, to give to you, and to care for you. And God will bring more and more things to you to be grateful for as you let go and as you go deeper. Gratitude is a very important quality that needs to be with you as you walk through your whole transformation. You should always have gratitude at the forefront of your mind: "Yes, I'm going through deep trans-formation, but I'm grateful, and I have so many things to be grateful for. I am grateful for just the fact that I'm going through this type of transformation that's setting me free." Then start to take a look at all that God has given you in your life. Gratitude is very important.

I want to end this talk with saying to you that you have to always remember that it is you, yourself, that must find the truth. You have to rely on your own awareness to go within and to experi-ence the truth directly. That is one reason that it is very important for you to have spiritual guidance from a master. The guidance gives you a hint at where to go within to find the truth. The guidance gives you very big hints about the illusion, so that you can go within and sort through the light and the dark within yourself. Then you can come to perceive truth directly for your-self, freedom for yourself, God for yourself, self realization in yourself. You can come to directly perceive Home, because you *are* Home; endless love, because it *is* endless. You come to per-ceive all of it because you directly realize it. There will be no more separation between you and God, or between you and you.

You need to have patience while not being complacent on the path. If you are complacent, you won't break through the illu-sion. If you don't have patience, you will drive yourself into a state that is counterproductive. You need to push forward *and* have patience. And you need to have gratitude.

You need to give up trying to figure out what I am talking about when I say "breaking free," "ultimate freedom," "union with God." If you are serious, then move a step closer every day. Sometimes "a step closer" means you are going to face a deeper level of illusion and darkness in order to bring more light to yourself.

You have to give up all of your concepts of what "a step closer" means. Every day, do everything that you can do to become freer, to move forward, to come closer to truth. Become freer and freer every day until the day arrives that you are filled with the presence of God. Become freer and freer until you stand in this world with the full presence and love of God in truth. Become freer and freer until you stand as someone who can help others to find freedom because you *know* freedom. You know it because you have directly found that reality, and that is the only true reality. You are not going to understand that until you directly realize it.

So don't form concepts from trying to understand anything that I am saying. Just take all of the words and use the words as a direction to guide you within. Take all of the words and feel the force that is pulling you within and calling you to come. There is a true hearing in you that can hear me when I say *"Come."* Freedom is waiting, even though you don't understand what that means and you're frustrated. Don't try to understand. Just do the spiritual work and never give up.

# Go to Sleep in Prayer

*spoken on April 9, 1996*

There is a very basic spiritual practice that you can incorporate into your life. You learn this practice at the very onset of your transformation of opening up to God, letting go, going through the trials and tribulations of surrendering to God.

In order for you to take it up as a spiritual practice, it is something that requires your conscious mind to really grasp hold of. It can help you in your daily life far beyond what you can comprehend with your mind. It is one of the most powerful things that you can do. It does not take any extra time in your life, but it requires consciousness and focus and desire. The more conscious your day is, the more desire you have during the day. (I do not mean frantic out-of-hand desire, but just deep-in-your-heart desire and movement forward in consciousness every day.) The more consciousness, desire, awareness, and prayer you have throughout the day while you are awake, the more natural and easy it will be for you to embrace this principle.

The practice is that every single night, as you are falling asleep, fall asleep in consciousness. To do that, fall asleep in a state of prayer, deep prayer. As you are drifting off to sleep, your last remembrances are of prayer. It takes a little bit of time to really have this practice become very natural in your life, but at a certain point, it will. You will just automatically go to sleep in such deep prayer, because so much movement went on during the day for you that the movement is just continuing when you sleep. As you fall asleep, you are just actually going into a place where the conscious mind is sleeping, but you are moving spiritually very quickly while you rest your body.

While you sleep, you can move spiritually, so quickly through so much, because of the help from God that can be with you while you are sleeping. Fall asleep in a conscious state of prayer to God. Pray to Him to help you, to work with you, to move you forward while you sleep. If you fall asleep with that prayer in your heart and with consciousness, the movement that you will have is very, very great. This is because your conscious mind isn't stopping anything when you are asleep. God can just work with you and move you while you sleep.

This teaching of going to sleep in a prayerful state isn't just a lightweight suggestion. It is a major meditation practice.

When you really take up this practice, in the beginning you may find that it is actually difficult to remain conscious while you are falling asleep. I remember when I started this practice, when Gourasana first spoke of it. I remember nights in a row lying there for hours. I couldn't fall asleep while I was conscious, because my consciousness was keeping me awake. But slowly the practice began to integrate. I began to get used to feeling prayer and begging God, "Please take me fast while I sleep. Wake me up different." And I was praying to the Heavenly Host of Light Beings. My prayer wouldn't be just to God, and I wouldn't call on Gourasana yet, but I could feel the Host of Light Beings. I somehow knew they were there. So while I was praying to God, I was asking for the Heavenly Host to work with me spiritually at night while I was asleep. So by the next day, I moved through so much illusion and woke up a different person.

Fast spiritual movement really does happen when you enter into this bedtime meditation. The power of the Incarnation and the Heavenly Host is very great, and They[1] do work with you while you sleep. The more conscious your prayer is as you are falling asleep, the more movement will happen to you while you sleep. So you see, it does not take any more time out of your life, but it is using your sleep time while you are resting to have an incredible several hours of deep meditation. When you wake up in the morning, you may not know what happened to you; but as your day starts to go on, you start to recognize increased awareness and a different feeling about you. You will see how powerful this practice is as you start to use it. This is a very basic, simple teaching. Incorporate it into your life just like you drink water or eat food.

When I say, "Go to sleep in prayer," I don't mean kneeling by your bed with your hands in prayer as you were taught when you were a child; I mean lying in bed with prayer in your consciousness. It doesn't matter if there are thoughts going on in your mind. The thoughts will go and go and go, but your overall thought, your overall consciousness keeps returning to "God, just take me. While I am sleeping, please move me fast."

Let yourself feel the power and the greatness of the Heavenly Host. Even though it sounds weird, some part of you can feel the Light Beings. As you start to pray to God, as you are open and you drift off to sleep, you will start to feel yourself mov-

---

[1] See Glossary at the back of the book: The Heavenly Host of Light Beings.

ing. Sometimes you will even wake up at night feeling different feelings. You may even wake up at night in a state of fear. This is because, when you are sleeping, you are sometimes working on a level of consciousness that is practically too much for your conscious mind, so when your conscious mind clicks in, you wake up in fear, even terror.

If you ever find yourself waking up in fear in the middle of the night, know that it is not a bad thing. It is just because the spiritual movement becomes too much for your conscious mind while you are asleep, so you get startled. You might wake up and find yourself sitting up, just afraid and a little disoriented. That is sometimes just how it is when God is working with you at night. But most of the time, you will just "conk" out in a state of prayer.

It is not a frantic state, or a state of anxiety, that you should fall asleep in. It is a peaceful prayer of desire. Let yourself be at peace as you are falling asleep into your sleep meditation, into your nighttime hours of meditation with God. Let yourself fall asleep in peace, even though the day may have been very frantic. Let there be peace as you are falling asleep. Within that peace, there is a desire and a very deep prayer, "God, take me fast while I sleep."[2]

Sometimes you will have dreams and sometimes no dreams. Sometimes you will wake up in the morning and feel like you definitely got run over by a Mack truck, or a Mack train – or maybe a Mack jet ran into you. You feel so altered and so different that you can't quite figure out who you are while you

---

[2] When Kalindi says, "God, take me fast while I sleep," this is a prayer asking to be moved while sleeping, to come into God as fast as possible. It is not a prayer to hasten death in any way. Kalindi teaches that coming fully into God must happen while you are alive.

are brushing your teeth in the morning. It takes some hours to integrate the new awareness and consciousness that happened to you while you were asleep.

So much goes on with you while you sleep at night. I cannot encourage you enough to take up this spiritual practice of going to sleep consciously praying for rapid movement while you sleep. Pray from a depth in your heart, and fall asleep with your last thought being "God, please take me fast." Falling asleep in a conscious state means falling asleep in a prayerful state of "Now I am going to rest and fall asleep, but I am going into my rest state with a conscious prayer for rapid movement." It is very powerful.

The more consciousness you develop and the more you fall asleep in a conscious state every night, the more you won't believe the results. Sometimes you will forget to do it, and that is okay; just do it as often as you can remember. Those of you who want to embrace it and really do it every night, put something by your bed that helps you remember to do it. You can always think about me – about Kalindi – if you can't figure out what to do. You can put a picture of Kalindi by your bed, and every time you look at that picture of Kalindi, you can remember to pray to God. You can remember about the Heavenly Host. You can remember about the Incarnation that has come to help you. You can look at a picture of Kalindi and remember my voice, and remember my urging you to pray as you fall asleep. Maybe there is a certain picture of Kalindi that you can have by your bed. Maybe you can do something with the picture every night. Maybe you can put a flower by it – or put a blanket over it! Do something with the picture every night that reminds you to crawl under your covers and fall asleep in prayer. When you are done with everything else – whether you are making love or whatever you are doing – have the last thing that you do before you fall asleep be deep prayer.

It doesn't matter how long you sleep; if you are someone that needs a long time of sleeping, that is okay. You may sleep for eight hours. You may sleep for ten hours. You may sleep for six hours. It is different for everyone. And it changes according to what is going on with you. But go to sleep in deep prayer so your whole sleep is about movement toward God. You will begin to wake up in the morning remembering that you went to sleep praying, and then your awareness throughout the day will start to open up more and more because of what happened to you while you were asleep.

I cannot stress to you enough the value and importance of this meditation practice, your sleep-time meditation. You can even tell your friends, or even people that aren't involved in the congregation or don't know anything about it. If they could learn the power of prayer as they fall asleep at night – that one thing – then their lives with God would start to change so much. So please try to hear. It is very powerful, so take up this practice.

What can I do but urge you and give you the tools? Live your day consciously, and go to sleep with conscious prayer, and rapid movement will be your daily life. This is one of the greatest tools that God has brought into conscious awareness for us to have. So please take it up. Find a way to remind yourself. I love you. Sweet dreams. Always fall asleep in prayer.

## NAMES OF PEOPLE

**David Swanson:** The man who allowed his body to be used for Gourasana to come into the world from 1987 until 1995, at which time the body died.

**Gourasana:** His name translates to mean "The Golden One." He is a current-day Incarnation of God. He comes directly from the Source.

**Kalindi:** A fully realized spiritual master for the world and the voice of God; Gourasana's first disciple, and His successor, along with The Lady.

**The Core:** The group of seven people who Gourasana worked with spiritually when He first came; they helped Gourasana found His Mission. They include Kalindi, The Lady, Jim St. James, Hana B. Mata, Marie, Candy, and Maha.

**The Lady:** Kalindi's first disciple and a fully realized spiritual master for the world; one of Gourasana's successors, along with Kalindi.

## TERMS

**Breaking the cycle of birth and death:** Refers to returning Home to God, taking no more birth. This spiritual state can only be achieved while a person is alive. Then at the natural time of death of the body, the soul fully returns Home. Kalindi also calls this "ultimate union with God" or "ultimate freedom." Sometimes Kalindi uses the term *true* enlightenment, because the term "enlightenment" is often misused.

**Conscious departure:** Kalindi's teaching about preparing for the time when your spirit leaves your body. Kalindi speaks that the ultimate conscious departure is returning to the spiritual realm at the natural time of death of the body, which means you have broken the cycle of birth and death while you are still alive. Or you can have conscious departure into the highest realm possible based on your consciousness at the time of your natural death. Suicide is *never* a conscious departure.

**Ego:** Illusion within a person; parts of the illusory self that cover over the true self. The ego is the false self, the illusory self, the being of illusion – that part of a person that is not real. Some examples of the ego are: unworthiness, arrogance, blame, resentment, hatred, anxiety, worry, fear, loneliness, guilt, shame.

**God, Source, Spirit, Father, All of Everything:** Kalindi uses many different names to refer to the Supreme Almighty. Although Kalindi often refers to God in the masculine, this reference is not meant to limit any notion of God's form, name, or gender.

**GMP:** The abbreviation for the Gourasana Meditation Practice, now called the Modern-Day Meditation. *(See Modern-Day Meditation in this glossary.)*

**Heavenly Host of Light Beings:** Also called "the Host," "Light Beings," and "true selves." The large group of spiritual beings that came with Gourasana with the express purpose to help those who want to leave this material realm and return Home; they are bringing the love of God to people everywhere. When Gourasana spoke, He often referred to Himself along with this group as "We" or "Us." The presence of this group helps make it possible for Gourasana to bring in so much power, so much special assistance, and so much love into the planet.

**Illusion:** Refers to the material realm, the plane of existence of which the earth is a part. It also is used to refer to the actual force of darkness that works against the light.

**Mission:** The general term used to describe the varied forms of assistance being given as a direct result of Gourasana's coming to earth. Sometimes used to refer to the principal organization formed to accomplish His mission.

**Modern-Day Meditation:** The Modern-Day Meditation is a unique practice with which one can go within, open and heal the heart, connect deeply with Source, and achieve both material and spiritual well-being. The meditation was first named the Gourasana Meditation Practice ("GMP") after Gourasana, who created it to help with all aspects of modern living, including the needs of body, mind, heart, and spirit. The Modern-Day Meditation is also referred to as the "Meditation for This Age" because it will remain a powerful practice for this age of the next 2,000 years of awakening.

The Modern-Day Meditation has four parts or components. The components are opening the emotional body, calming, thinking, and going into action. When Kalindi says, "hit the floor," or "floor work," or talks about "screaming" or "crying" in meditation, she is referring to Part One of this meditation: opening the emotional body. It is common to start the meditation practice by sitting on the floor.

**path:** A "path" is each person's personal spiritual journey.

**Path:** The "Path" refers to The Path to Ultimate Freedom founded by Kalindi based on Gourasana's teachings. It is designed to help people break the cycle of birth and death in this lifetime, and to help people come closer to the love of God and get freer and freer from the illusion every day.

**Special assistance:** Due to the unusually large number of souls that want to return Home at this time, this is specific spiritual help from this Incarnation of God, Gourasana, and the Heavenly Host. The transformational energy is a part of the special assistance. The special assistance helps people move forward at a rapid enough speed to be able to succeed in spiritual transformation; the speed of spiritual transformation has never been as fast as it is now with this assistance. The special assistance is also working night and day all over the world in a global effort to help all of humankind with the illusory force that is holding back love.

**True realm of existence:** Also called the "true realm" or "Home." It refers to the spiritual realm or the spiritual plane of existence. The spiritual plane is where the soul resides with God.

**True self:** The soul, the part of you that is always connected to God.

**True self manifestation:** The process of the soul, the true self, returning Home to God, while one is still living on earth in a body. Lifetime after lifetime a being of illusion is created that covers over the true self. True self manifestation happens as the true self lets go of these layers of illusion and emerges, standing in this material world in union with God, living in God's will. This is Kalindi's term for *true* enlightenment.

**Transformational energy:** The benevolent spiritual power from God through the Host to help you break free of illusion. This energy started in the 1960's; it is available throughout the world in full power now and is felt increasingly around the world. Gourasana let it be known how to work with this energy.

We are overjoyed to be able to offer you Kalindi's spoken words in writing and hope that you find great benefit from them.

We wish to express our heartfelt thanks to the many people who worked on this project with dedication and devotion to preserving Kalindi's words.

Jayden Inglis and Sherri Montgomery helped to review and edit Kalindi's words. Thank you to Claus Pfitzner, Ámundi Sigurðsson, and Minka St. James for design; to Christine Vlachos, Ed DeRosis, Laura Barnum, Diane Walker-Allison, Mark Christie, and Andra Joyce-Higa for proofreading; and to Leslie McDonald for management and production.

Tamara La Toto and Kendra Davis
Editors

Kalindi was born in 1955. From the age of 18, she was a spiritual seeker. Her quest took her to Israel, where she had a pull in her heart to visit the place where Jesus walked, the Sea of Galilee. Here she had a profound spiritual awakening. This pull to connect to Jesus was quite surprising to her, because Kalindi grew up in the Jewish religion.

Upon returning to the US, Kalindi met her first spiritual master, Srila Prabhupada. He introduced her to the path of bhakti yoga, which means love and devotion to God.

After years of austerity, love, and joy, Kalindi met David Swanson. They had had a very strong spiritual partnership for ten years before Lord Gourasana made His presence known to them. David and Kalindi, along with a core group of six others, recognized Gourasana as the Father Almighty – a modern-day Incarnation of God. This Core – The Lady, Jim, Hana, Marie, Candy, and Maha – then began their spiritual transformations.

Today, because of David's surrender, Lord Gourasana coming to this world, Kalindi becoming the Voice of God and Spiritual Master for the World, and the Core's never-ending support, the Mission of Gourasana is growing throughout the world. Having fulfilled her destiny, Kalindi passed in April 2010. The Lady now leads Gourasana's worldwide Mission, known as Center of The Golden One, that is dedicated to helping people get freer and closer to the love of God.

Kalindi's teachings are available through the Center of The Golden One®. The Center, founded in 1991, was named after a current-day Incarnation of God, Lord Gourasana, The Golden One. The Center has a worldwide network of centers and communities that offer meditations and spiritual programs to help people come closer to God. Kalindi's books, lectures, and DVD's are available through the Center's bookstore and online. The following offerings are a way to learn about Kalindi's teachings:

**Love's Awakening**ᔆᴹ: Powerful spiritual seminars to guide people within to wake up their consciousness, discover the truth of who they truly are, and experience an undeniable connection to God.

**Modern-Day Meditation**®: A unique practice that helps with the well-being of body, mind, heart, and spirit. With this meditation one can go within, release emotions, then naturally calm and think in prayerful contemplation to gain information about taking action to achieve both spiritual and material success in this current age.

**Freedom Walk**ᔆᴹ: A wide variety of offerings for spiritual transformation including meditations, programs, workshops, spiritual coaching, and social activities.

**Path to Ultimate Freedom**®: Rapid-speed spiritual transformation for those who want to break the cycle of birth and death in this lifetime and achieve full union with God.

## UPDATED INFORMATION

Center of The Golden One
4277 West 43rd Avenue
Denver, Colorado, 80212
303-800-0782
CenterofTheGoldenOne.com

CENTER OF
**THE GOLDEN ONE**

There is a spiritual Seminar available through
Center of The Golden One®
that can facilitate direct realization of your
own personal connection to God
and profound and radical movement in your
spiritual transformation,
no matter what path you are traveling.

Also available are audio talks and books
on spiritual transformation and the
Gourasana Meditation Practice® (GMP®) –
a powerful meditation practice
for this current age.
You are welcome whatever your faith,
religion, or spiritual practice.

74352190R00136

Made in the USA
Columbia, SC
30 July 2017